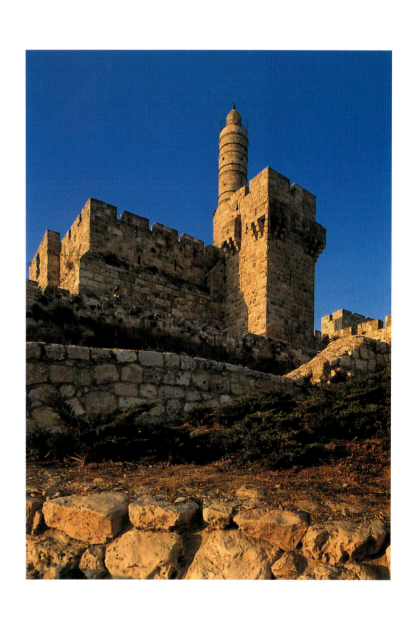

PLACES israel AND HISTORY

Texts
Annie Sacerdoti

Editing supervision by
Valeria Manferto De Fabianis

Art director
Patrizia Balocco Lovisetti

Graphic design by
Anna Galliani

Translation
C.T.M., Milan

1 David's Citadel is one of the most interesting sites in the old city: it is certainly a very beautiful example of civil architecture but, more importantly, it houses the Museum of the History of Jerusalem which illustrates the history of the city from the Canaanite period to the modern day.

2/7 The citadel of Jerusalem has fascinated generations of travelers in the Holy Land, including the Scottish painter David Roberts, who left to posterity drawings such as this one made in 1839, which shows the fortress near the Gate of Jaffr.

3/6 The ancient city of Jerusalem is still surrounded by Ottoman walls and is truly one of the wonders of the world. Inside the walls the city is divided into four quarters: Armenian, Moslem, Christian and Jewish. Each quarter has its own churches, mosques or synagogues in such numbers and of such importance as to affirm that Jerusalem is without doubt the holiest city in the world.

© 1998, 2007 White Star s.p.a.
Via C. Sassone 22/24
13100 Vercelli, Italy
New updated edition

All Rights Reserved. No part of this book may be reproduced in any form or by any means without the written permission of the publisher.
White Star Publishers® is a registered trademark property of White Star s.p.a.

ISBN 13: 978-88-544-0319-2

1 2 3 4 5 6   11 10 09 08 07

Printed in China.

CONTENTS

INTRODUCTION	PAGE	8
A YOUNG COUNTRY WITH THOUSANDS OF YEARS OF HISTORY	PAGE	18
THE PLACES WHERE THE PAST IS WRITTEN	PAGE	54
A SMALL LAND OF A THOUSAND COLORS	PAGE	74
JERUSALEM, CENTER OF THREE WORLD RELIGIONS	PAGE	96
CITIES FROM THE BIBLE AND CITIES OF THE FUTURE	PAGE	110
A SINGLE PEOPLE OF A THOUSAND FACES	PAGE	124
INDEX	PAGE	132

INTRODUCTION

8 top left The surface of the Dead Sea (368 sq. miles) is falling due to loss from evaporation that is not replaced by equal quantities of water. The sea is divided into two parts at HaLashon by a strip of land cut by a canal.

8 top right The Negev Desert occupies 60 per cent of the whole of Israel. Its landscape is one of the most attractive in the country for its geological formations and many deep wadis.

8-9 The Jordan valley is by far the most heavily cultivated area of Israel. Even sections of barren, desert land and malarial swamps have been transformed into green countryside thanks to new techniques of cultivation and irrigation. However, over 35 per cent of Israel's land, 2,820 square miles, is still defined as "uncultivated and non-productive."

9 top Wadis are waterways in the desert, completely dry for long periods but that suddenly fill in winter when it rains. Then the torrents wash away everything in their path.

9 bottom The octagonal Sanctuary of the Beatitudes was designed and built in 1937 by the architect Barluzzi. One of the eight Beatitudes is depicted on each interior wall and symbols of the seven virtues are represented on the flooring. The building is surrounded by a portico which gives marvellous views over Lake Tiberias. The place is venerated in memory of Jesus' Sermon on the Mount.

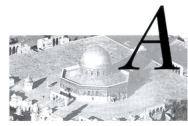

A journey to Israel is something special, unique, out of the ordinary and not always easy. In a tiny area, a fraction smaller than Wales, there are many different types of landscape: there is the sandy coastline, meticulously cultivated valleys, snow-topped mountains, arid deserts, fish-filled fresh-water lakes, the salt-water Dead Sea, and the miraculously intact coral reef in the Red Sea.

Against this varied backdrop, in the modern cities covering a large part of the Mediterranean coastline we find skyscrapers which contrast with some of the oldest sites of human habitation in the world.

Their ruins bear witness to ancient civilizations that over the centuries fought one another, superseded one another or lived together, though often with strong contrasts.

Israel is therefore an ideal destination for travelers of many types. Those who go in search of their Christian roots only have to walk through the streets and tour the churches, monasteries and holy sites of Bethlehem, Nazareth and Tiberius, bathe in the waters of the river Jordan or go to Jerusalem to find the answers to their questions, so mystical and conducive to meditation these places are.

The traveller who is fascinated by the evolution of the many civilizations that developed and succeeded one another has only to visit the many archaeological sites, museums and exhibitions; the wide range of choice is likely to cause some embarrassment, as archaeology is almost a national pastime, a collective passion. Everybody searches for the certainties of the ancient past, perhaps to assuage the uncertainties of the present. You can visit Jericho, considered the oldest city in the world, or retrace the routes of the Nabatean caravans that in the 2nd century BC founded stop-over points in the Negev desert at Shivta, Mamshit and Avdat for travelers from Petra to Gaza on the Mediterranean coast. Remains of Roman domination can be seen at the forts of Hero-

10 top left These arcades date from the Crusader era. They stand in the Roman and medieval section of Caesarea. The city became famous for its large port, built between 37 and 34 BC at Herod the Great's wish. The city was chosen to be the capital of Roman Palestine. Its architectural remains make it one of Israel's most interesting sites.

10-11 This perfectly preserved 3rd century synagogue can be seen at Bar Am in Galilee.

11 top left There are many forts in Israel, like Yechiam in the photograph. They were mostly built during the Crusades as support and supply points for the Christian troops and as a barrier against Moslem advances.

11 top right Bet She'an has been a relatively important city at different periods of the region's history from as early as 3000 BC. The site was conquered by David and later became Scythopolis, a large Roman city with remains still to be seen: these include an amphitheater, colonnaded streets and public buildings.

10 bottom left The synagogue of Hammat, near Tiberias, built in the 3rd-4th century AD on the ruins of preceding buildings, was destroyed at the end of the 4th century. It was then rebuilt in the form of a basilica, with naves decorated with mosaics.

10 right Bet She'arim was the central village on a farming property belonging to Berenice, great-grandchild of Herod the Great. Today its remains can be visited.

dion and Masada or in the ancient port of Ashkelon. At Kapharnoum, on the northern bank of Lake Tiberius, there are traces of the Roman Via Maris which went as far as Syria; and nearby, at Bet Shearim, the amazing necropolises can be visited.

In the same area, at Hammat Gader, the visitor can see the Roman baths and ancient synagogue; the 3rd century synagogue at Bar Am is one of the best preserved buildings in Galilee. Then of course there is Caesarea where the Roman period found its best expression: the aqueduct and theater there are practically intact.

The Crusaders too left the country indelible reminders of their passing. In northern Galilee there is the grandest and best preserved castle in the country, the castle of Montfort; in Golan there is the largest one, the castle of Nimrud; and in the Jordan valley the well equipped castle of Belvoir, one of the few that Saladin did not manage to conquer. Neither did the Byzantines fail to leave their mark; for example, there are the mosaics of the synagogue at Bet Alpha, to the south of Nazareth, which reproduce vineshoots and geometric patterns; then there are reminders of the era of the Caliphs, with the palace of Hisham built by Abd-el-Malik (724-743 AD) to the north of Jericho. However, the Israelis may be more interested in their own remote past as represented by the Dead Sea scrolls written in the 1st century BC found at Qumran and now kept in the Israel Museum in Jerusalem, or perhaps by the mosaics illustrating animals and flowers in a 5th-6th century synagogue at Ein Ghedi, an oasis in the desert.

In this small land, where nature plays such an important part, the visitor enters a unique atmosphere, a history marked by the passage of prophets and bandits, heroes and hermits, where the peoples speak a babel of languages and follow different customs and religions but all share a single drive - to live freely in the Land of the Fathers as though six thousand years of history had not taken place. It is this atmosphere, which cannot be found anywhere else on earth, that moves and rouses the inhabitants and visitors and leaves nobody indifferent. A journey round Israel thus becomes a pilgrimage to places of the past and the present but also a visit to the three great monotheistic religions and many sects that have flowered in the mystical atmosphere Israel engenders. It becomes a journey to a world of national and social ideologies, a journey into history and the world of the Bible. On the way the visitor learns of experiments like the kibbutz, and the social and political problems created by the coexistence of different peoples who, for different reasons, all claim the right to live on the same patch of land. This is a journey into one's own self, into one's own soul and one's most intimate feelings. This is why every time you visit Israel it is always like being there for the first time.

The Dead Sea Salt Beds.

Rosh Hanigra and the Mediterranean Sea.

Majdal Shams and Mount Hermon.

14-15 The red projections of the fortress of Masada on the Dead Sea are still a powerful symbol of the history of the Jews. After Jerusalem was conquered by the Romans, a thousand men, women and children, shut themselves in this fort built by Herod the Great on the top of the mountain. When they realized they could not resist the siege of the Roman soldiers, they preferred mass suicide to capture.

16-17 Caesarea was built by Herod between 37 and 34 BC at the place of an ancient anchorage known as the Tower of Stratone. The Romans then built a port on the site able to give shelter to hundreds of vessels, then surrounded the port with a city. The amphitheater has been rebuilt and today the seats become filled with spectators once again for cultural events and shows.

Eilat and the Red Sea.

Mizpe Ramon and the Desert of Zin.

A YOUNG LAND WITH THOUSANDS OF YEARS OF HISTORY

18 left The bone tool with the handle in the shape of an animal head was found by archaeologists in the caves at el-Wad. It is one of the objects held in the Israel Museum in Jerusalem that experts attribute to the Natufian culture, from roughly 8,000 years ago.

It all began in the arc that stretches from the Tigris and Euphrates rivers as far as the Sinai, between the Mediterranean and the desert of the Arabian peninsula. It has been called the fertile half-moon, the fertile crescent and the fertile scythe, all of which refer to its shape. Ten thousand years ago, when Europe had still not come out of the last Ice Age, it was here that man discovered that barley and wheat could be cultivated near villages and that it was not necessary to go in search of them. Eight thousand years ago Jericho was built, the first city-fortress in the world, able to house three thousand inhabitants. And it was here that man learnt to bake bread and fire clay in brick ovens. Later, roughly five thousand years ago, man discovered that by baking malachite collected from the desert rocks he was able to produce copper. He also learnt to translate his ideas into hieroglyphs; the oldest known evidence of writing is a tablet 3,500 years old found at Qish on the banks of the Euphrates. It was the breeding ground of human civilization and it was here that the roots of the history of Israel are to be found.

Around the year 2000 BC, groups of nomads and semi-nomads from Mesopotamia (today Iraq and Syria) moved in successive stages towards the coast of the Mediterranean where the city-states of the Canaanites flourished: Hazor, Megiddo, Bet She'an, Sheshem, Gezer and Jerusalem. The strangers were known as *hapiru* or *habiru*. They looked for pastures for their herds and occasionally offered their services as mercenaries. The name appears in several Canaanite and Egyptian texts and, given the assonance, it has been theorized that they were the first Hebrews (Jews). The people who compiled the Bible recorded that their patriarchs had been *gerim* (strangers) in the land of Canaan. Year after year the wanderers moved further on despite the opposition from locals, though at times the two intermixed. The nomadic groups ended by establishing small settlements based on *beth-ab* (the house of the father) in which the head of the family held absolute power.

18 right The two statuettes, one male and one female, are held in the Israel Museum in Jerusalem. They are carved from hippopotamus teeth. There are several holes in the head of the male figure which would have held locks of hair. Both statuettes were discovered in the Negev Desert, though the exact location is known only of the male figure - Be'er-Safad-Be'er Matar near Beersheba.

*19 top left
This funerary urn, 20 inches tall, was used to hold the bones of the dead in a secondary tomb. It dates from the middle of the 4th century BC and comes from an area south of Jaffa called Hazor, known as Holon today.*

The decoration of stylized animals is common to ossuaries found in the same area. The urn is in the Israel Museum in Jerusalem.

*19 top right
The copper scepter decorated with the heads of ibex, made during the Copper Age, was found in the "Treasure Cave" at Nahal Mishmar in the Judaean Desert, where it was wrapped in reed-matting with 429 other objects and buried.*

19 bottom This copper scepter has no handle and is decorated with the heads of two ibex. It has been perfectly preserved by the dryness of the Judaean Desert where it was found buried with many other objects from the Copper Age (4th millennium BC).

20 The painting shows Noah's Ark and the clearing of the rain clouds. It is attributed to a painter of the French School of the 15th century and held in the British Library in London. Noah is considered the archetype of the just man; he obeyed the order from God to build an ark and take aboard a pair of every kind of animal to save them from the Flood, providing them with proper food day and night.

It is against this background that figures such as Abraham, Isaac and Jacob, the patriarchs, emerged. The stories that have grown up around them are so incoherent as to put their existence, as history has passed it down to us, in doubt. More likely is that they were chiefs, forefathers or founders of tribes that lived in phases over a period of time in the land of Canaan before settling there permanently. The Jews also brought their religion to Canaan, based on the "god of the fathers," understood first to mean the god of one's own father and then, more remotely, the god of all one's forefathers.

It was a religion tied to people rather than to places or nature (mountains, rivers, trees, etc.), unlike that of the Canaanites. It was based on divine protection of the patriarch of the clan and the clan itself and not on fixed places, therefore it was more suited to a semi-nomadic society in contrast to the stability of the Canaanite population.

And if it is true that the cult of the patriarchs was later assimilated into the cult and the temples of Canaan, the fundamental concept of the god of the fathers, which had nothing to do with polytheism, endured and later developed into the actual religion of the Jewish people.

21 top This oil painting is by the painter Domenichino (Domenico Zampieri, 1581-1641) and hangs in the Prado, in Madrid. It shows Abraham's sacrifice. Abraham is the model of the law-abiding Jew faithful to the will of God. He was a prophet and priest and passed the many tests set him, such as the sacrifice of his son Isaac, to prove his faith in God. The story is told in the Book of Genesis.

21 bottom This picture by the Renaissance master Raphael (1483-1520) is housed in the Vatican Museum in Rome. It depicts the Flight of Jacob into Egypt. It was painted between 1515 and 1518. The Bible tells the story of Jacob's long flight to Egypt in the Book of Genesis; together with his sons. Jacob is considered the forefather of the Jewish people.

Toward the end of the 13th century BC, perhaps during the reign of the Egyptian pharaoh Seti I (1304-1290 BC), groups of Jews moved into Egypt, probably forced by famine. The Bible tells us that the sons of Jacob were sent to search for corn and found their brother Joseph who had been sold into slavery to the Egyptians and who had become advisor to the pharaoh. As a matter of fact, movements of groups of people in one direction or another as a result of famine or war were frequent

and it is almost certain that Semitic tribes had previously been to Egypt, "the land of Zoan," at the delta of the Nile.

The tranquil existence of the Jews in Egypt lasted until a pharaoh ascended to the throne who "had not known Joseph" and who forced them into slavery. It was under Ramesses II and maybe his successor, Merneptah, that the Jews left Egypt. This was the episode that the Bible calls the Exodus. We do not know if the Jews escaped or were expelled from Egypt. Perhaps both things occurred, at different times for different groups. The group that the Bible says was led by Moses went into the Sinai to reach the Promised Land, i.e., Canaan. The group remained in the desert for a period which was of major importance to history because it was then that the Jewish religion took on the connotations that characterize it today and that the bonds which link the religion so strongly to the Jewish people were established.

22 top left This picture by Raphael (1483-1520) hangs in the Vatican Museum in Rome. It depicts Joseph interpreting the dreams of the Pharaoh of Egypt. The story of Joseph is told in the book of Genesis; it describes his flight into Egypt, his imprisonment and his release due to the intervention of the Pharaoh, who asked Joseph to interpret the dreams that no wise man or prophet had been able to explain.

22-23 *The painter Julius Schnorr von Carolsfeld (1794-1874) illustrated the construction of pyramids by the Jews held as slaves in Egypt. The work was colored at a later date and is one of the 240 wood engravings used in the "Illustrated Bible" that the German artist edited between 1825 and 1860 on his return to Germany after a long stay in Rome.*

23 *The gilded pendant with the stylized engraving of the head of a woman shows strong Egyptian influences. The head is probably of Asthoreth, the goddess of fertility, who is linked to the Egyptian deity Hathor, protectress of women, noted for her love of music and as a guardian of the dead. The pendant was found at Tell el-Ajjul and is displayed in the Israel Museum in Jerusalem. It dates from the Bronze Age (c. 3150 – 1200 BC).*

22 bottom *The fresco by Raphael (1483-1520) is part of the cycle he created between 1515 and 1518 in the Vatican loggias in Rome. It shows the Jews crossing the Red Sea. The flight from Egypt and the end of slavery are celebrated each year with the feast of Pesach (the Jewish Easter) and are narrated in the Book of Exodus.*

24 top This fresco decorates the vault of Anagni Cathedral: it shows the Philistines with the Ark of the Covenant. The legend goes that the Ark was placed in the first Temple on the foundation stone on which the world was created. Jewish tradition says that the Ark was not destroyed when the Temple was conquered in 587 BC but was hidden and will remain so until the coming of the Messiah.

24 bottom This is another episode taken from the fresco in the vault of Anagni Cathedral and depicts the defeat of the Philistines by the Israelis at the battle of Mizpah. The Philistines were a "sea people" which landed on the shores of Canaan at the end of the 13th century BC. They were settled in the southern coastal region for almost two centuries and organized in small city-states. They were definitively defeated and subjected by King David.

24-25 This painting by Nicolas Poussin (1594-1665) shows Joshua's victory over the Ammonites.

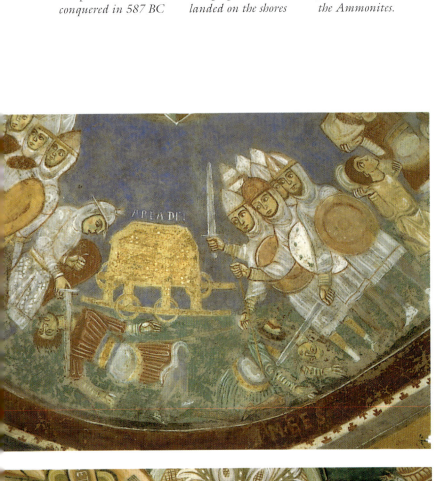

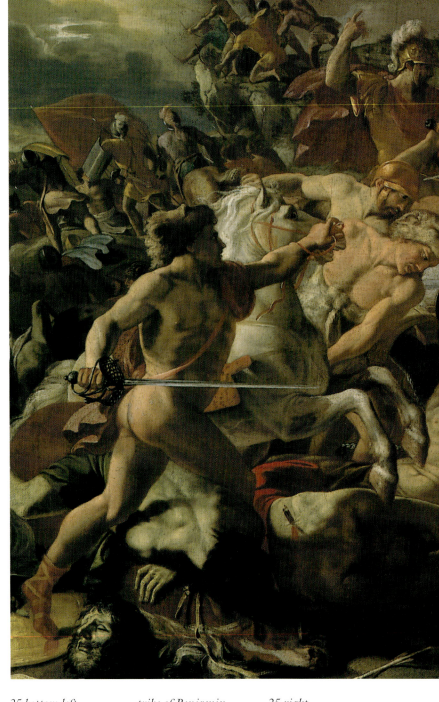

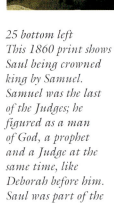

25 bottom left This 1860 print shows Saul being crowned king by Samuel. Samuel was the last of the Judges; he figured as a man of God, a prophet and a Judge at the same time, like Deborah before him. Saul was part of the tribe of Benjamin, famous for its warriors, and was the first king of Israel (c. 1060-1007 BC). He killed himself at the battle of Gilboa when he was surrounded by Philistines. He was succeeded by his son-in-law, David.

25 right This drawing on parchment from the Byzantine era is held in the Bibliothèque Nationale in Paris. It shows the coronation of David as king of the Hebrews. David succeeded in uniting the twelve tribes of Israel into a single kingdom (1000-970 BC). Jerusalem, a Jebusite city, became the capital and spiritual center of the Hebrew people.

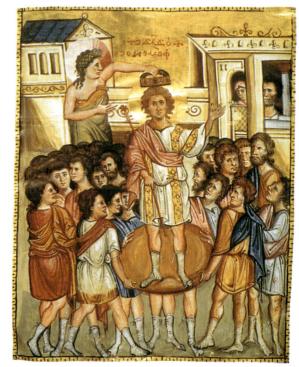

The Bible refers to the many battles fought by the Israelites under the leadership of Joshua to gain the Promised Land but in fact what occurred was no more than a mainly peaceful penetration further inland. It should not be forgotten that the Canaanites and the Jews spoke similar languages, that many cities were shared by the two peoples and that there were many mixed marriages, as the Bible tells us.

Other peoples were much more hostile, such as the Ammonites, Edomites, Amalekites and, in particular, the Philistines who had probably originated in Cyprus and Anatolia and then moved to the coastal regions (which consequently took on the name Palestine). The Jews were divided into tribes (Judah, Simeon, Reuben, Manasseh, Ephraim, Gad, Dan, Benjamin, Asher, Naphtali, Zebulun, and Issachar) and spread across the area. They met up when they had to confront enemies, for which purpose they would name an outright leader (Judge). In 1020 BC, the last of the Judges, Samuel, was succeeded by Saul, the first king of Israel.

The unity of the kingdom hardly lasted a century during which Saul was succeeded on the throne by David, Solomon and Rehoboam.

26 top This 13th-century French miniature shows King Solomon studying the Torah. Solomon's reputation for wisdom and knowledge spread far beyond the borders of his country as proven by the visit of the Queen of Sheba, who visited from southern Arabia to meet the king of Israel. Solomon's learning was considered the "greatest of all the sons of the Orient."

26 bottom At the apex of his power and prestige, Solomon built a large Temple in Jerusalem, here reproduced from a valuable Haggadah published in Bohemia in 1728-29. The construction of the Temple was described copiously in the Bible in the Book of Kings.

26-27 Solomon was the son of David and Bathsheba. In this picture he is shown on the throne in two different instances. Famous for his wisdom, he transformed the kingdom (970 – 928 BC) into a single, centralized and bureaucratic state. Solomon has been attributed authorship of the Books of Proverbs and Ecclesiastes in the Bible and the Song of Songs.

Only under the reign of Solomon did the country succeed in becoming a real military and economic power. Solomon increased trade with nearby peoples, subjected others from whom he received sizeable tributes, established a solid alliance with Egypt and the kings of Tyre (in modern day Lebanon) and built the large temple in Jerusalem. On his death, the ten tribes of the north rebelled, probably as a result of the high taxes and excessive centralization of power in the capital, and they created their own kingdom under Jeroboam. The end for this kingdom came one hundred years later, due to internal fighting and the rise of a powerful force on its borders, the Assyrians. In 720 BC, King Sargon II conquered the country and deported most of its people. The country to the south, Judaea, with Jerusalem as its capital, survived little more than another hundred years when another power, this time the Babylonians, invaded in 597 BC and they too deported many of the inhabitants. Ten years later, King Nebuchadnezzar II destroyed Jerusalem and Solomon's temple.

This collapse, which also caused the first great Diaspora, has always been considered a turning point in the history of the Jews, so much so that even today it is remembered with three days of fasting each year. On the tenth day of 'teveth' (December-January) the siege of Jerusalem began; on the seventeenth day of 'tamuz' (June-July) the temple was destroyed; on the third day of 'tishrì' (September-October) Ghedalià, the governor left in Jerusalem by the Babylonians, was killed at the hands of his fellow-citizens. This episode also represented a turning point for the conception of Judaism: the original link with the Promised Land remained but the Jews understood that they would only be able to survive as a people with their culture and tradition intact by safeguarding at any cost their one unifying element, their religious identity.

27 top This 13th-century manuscript represents the conquest of Jerusalem, the deporting of the Jews to Babylon and three couples of Christ's forefathers. Recent excavations in Israel support the theory that the destruction of Jerusalem and the Babylonian exile did not completely empty Israel of its inhabitants. The biblical account in the Book of Jeremiah also states that Nebuchadnezzar left behind him a part of the poorest members of the population.

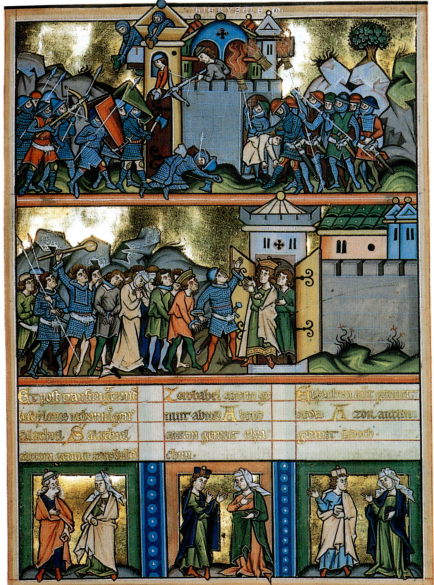

27 bottom A print from 1732 shows the city of Jerusalem at the time of the conquest by Nebuchadnezzar. The Book of Kings in the Old Testament tells that the city was besieged and surrounded on all sides by the Babylonian troops who destroyed all resistance and carried the inhabitants of Judaea away to captivity.

Fifty years later another foreign power changed the turn of events for the Jews. In 539 BC, Cyrus the Great, king of Persia, conquered Babylon and allowed the Jews to return to their homeland. Fifty thousand of them did so and, once back in Jerusalem, rebuilt the temple and reorganized the religious hierarchy and their theocratic state.

Two centuries later, Alexander the Great conquered Syria and Palestine. On his death in 323 BC his kingdom

28 top left Cyrus the Great allowed the Hebrews to return to the Promised Land, led by Sessbasar and Zorobabel, and strove to have the Temple of Jerusalem rebuilt in original its form. The engraving shows the work in progress and the instructions personally given by Cyrus.

28 bottom left This copper engraving by Matthaus Merian (1593-1650) shows Alexander the Great, king of Macedonia, receiving the keys to the city of Jerusalem from the high priest. When Alexander conquered Palestine in 332 BC, the population was almost entirely concentrated around Jerusalem.

28 top right This marble statue of Alexander the Great stands in the Acropolis Museum in Athens. It is a copy of a bronze statue made in the 1st century BC by Euphranor.

Alexander was the son of Philip II of Macedonia and was the pupil of Aristotle. It was his aim to create a universal empire by uniting Greece with eastern territories. His concept of Hellenism profoundly influenced the political and cultural thought of his time.

was divided among his generals and Palestine was given first to Ptolemy of Egypt and then, in 198 BC, to the Seleucids of Syria. Under the influence of Hellenism, the period was fecund for the cultures of the Mediterranean region and therefore for the Jews too who enjoyed a discreet religious and juridical autonomy. Knowledge of the Greek language and Greek philosophy spread; the Old Testament was translated into Greek by seventy wise men who met in Alexandria in Egypt, even if groups of local observers rejected this adhesion to a culture they considered foreign and therefore profane. Indeed, when king Antiochus IV Epiphanes started a more radical Hellenization of society, the Jews rebelled. Antiochus occupied Jerusalem, massacred the population and dedicated Solomon's temple to Jupiter. But the Jews were very determined: they reconquered the city, reconsecrated the temple and even managed to achieve a certain degree of religious and administrative autonomy.

28 bottom right Antiochus III Seleucid (223 – 187 BC), king of Syria, succeeded his brother Seleucus III and conquered Syria and Phoenicia at the end of the fifth Syrian war (202 – 201 BC). He was subsequently defeated by the Romans and died in 187 BC. History remembers him as a great patron and for the creation of the library in Antioch.

29 This illuminated French manuscript of the 15th century is part of a volume of chronicles by Jean de Coucy and is held in the Bibliothèque Nationale in Paris. It describes the sacking of the Temple's treasure and the transformation of Jerusalem into a Greek city with a gymnasium and school.

When high priest John Hyrcanus of the Hasmonean dynasty proclaimed himself king, Palestine once more became a kingdom and enjoyed eighty years of prosperity. In 67 BC, at the moment of succession to the throne, the clash between Pharisees, in favour of further Hellenization, and the Sadducees, in opposition to it, turned into civil war. The two candidates to the throne, Hyrcanus II and Aristobulus II, each asked for help from the ruler of the largest Mediterranean power at the time, Pompey of Rome, who was then in Damascus. The Roman general took full advantage of the situation: he captured Aristobulus, put Hyrcanus on the throne and turned Palestine into a vassal state.

From that moment on the Jews were no longer protagonists in their own history but simply the political tools of Rome and of the other powers which dominated the area over the following centuries. The last king with any degree of autonomy was Herod the Great. He was an admirer of Hellenism and of Rome and its

30 The Temple of Jerusalem was completely destroyed by the Roman army by order of Emperor Titus in AD 70. The soldiers removed the seven-branched candlestik, the menorah, as booty and the Jews were forced to leave the country as slaves. This bas-relief shows the famous picture from the Arch of Titus in Rome.

culture; he was a great builder and enriched the country with forts and palaces and rebuilt the temple in a very grand style. On his death in 4 BC, Rome took direct control of the country and established its own administration and governor. With the birth of Jesus at Bethlehem during Herod's reign came the origin of Christianity which was to revolutionize the world's views on religion.

30-31 This oil painting by French painter Nicolas Poussin (1594-1665) hangs in Vienna. It shows the destruction of the Temple of Jerusalem by Titus. Poussin was a great admirer of Titian and Raphael and spent 23 years in Rome supported by the collector Cassiano del Pozzo. He painted many pictures of classic mythological subjects and events from Roman history.

31 top This 15th-century miniature taken from an Italian Bible shows Christ taken before the tetrarch Herod Antipas. On Alexander the Great's death, his empire was divided into four sections and a tetrarch was appointed as governor of each one. Herod Antipas founded the town of Tiberias in honour of Emperor Tiberius.

31 bottom This bronze Roman coin was minted in celebration of the final conquest of Judaea and its designation as a Roman province. Judaea is shown as a woman defeated by another one, representing Rome. To defeat the Jews, the Romans had to mobilize three legions comprising a total of 60,000 men. The war ended with the destruction of the Temple of Jerusalem.

For Romans, Palestine proved to be the most unruly of the many provinces in their enormous empire. Roman domination started off a guerrilla warfare known as the Jewish War that was to last over one hundred years and cause the deaths of hundreds of thousands of people. This was despite Titus conquering Jerusalem in AD 70, destroying the temple and deporting tens of thousands of Jews. The most important event in this war was the strenuous resistance of the Jews at the fort of Masada on the Dead Sea against the

siege, and eventual victory, by the Romans. The Jews did not surrender to the enemy but preferred to commit suicide en masse.

In AD 135 Emperor Hadrian transformed Judaea into a real Roman colony called Syria Palestina. He changed the name of Jerusalem to Aelia Capitolina, destroyed Solomon's temple, built another one dedicated to Jupiter in its place and forbade Jews to stay in their own city. Once more the few Jews left turned to their religion to find the strength to survive. In the small communities in the desert they took up studies of the scriptures and wrote the Mishnah, the first great post-biblical collection of Jewish law, and completed the Halakah, the book of religious law, which had long been debated in academies. Those commentaries today make up the Talmud.

32 left This bronze bust is displayed in the Israel Museum in Jerusalem. It was found during excavations at Scythopolis near Bet She'an in Israel. It is of the Roman emperor Hadrian (AD 76 – 138). In 129 Hadrian visited Judaea which had been a Roman consular province for 10 years. Once the revolt of Bar-Kochba had been put down, he built Aelia Capitolina, a pagan city, on the ruins of Jerusalem.

32-33 The picture shows one of the Dead Sea scrolls found in 1947 at Qumran in Israel. The parchments are preserved at the Book Sanctuary in Jerusalem. They are written partly in Hebrew and partly in Aramaic and contain biblical texts and documents about the community at Qumran. They belonged to the Essenes, a religious sect founded during the 2nd century BC and destroyed during the first Jewish War.

33 left The Romans issued this coin during the time that Pontius Pilate governed Judaea (AD 26-36). The coin shows the curved stick that was the symbol of the Roman priest who forecast the future. The Jews considered it offensive to their religion to be forced to use coins depicting pagan symbols.

33 right This illuminated manuscript from the end of the 16th century portrays Vespasian with his son Titus. Head of the Flavian dynasty, Vespasian appointed his son co-ruler. Titus led the Roman troops that besieged and conquered Jerusalem in AD 70, destroying the Temple and taking Jewish slaves to Rome.

34 left This 17th-century Turkish miniature shows Mohammed in the cave with Abu Bakr. Mohammed (570 – 632) is considered the father of Islam. When in 610 he had a revelation and began the cycle of his monotheistic prophecies, he declared he did not want to eliminate the tradition of Israel but to enlarge it and accommodate it to the new divine decrees entrusted to him.

Over the following centuries the Jewish people became poorer and suffered, to the advantage of the Christian population supported by the Byzantines. The Jewish population in Palestine was diminished by constant emigrations, although small Jewish kingdoms and potentates sprang up on islands in the Strait of Tiran, along the Red Sea and even in south east Arabia.

In 638, just six years after the death of the prophet Mohammed, the Arabs reconquered Palestine overthrowing the Byzantine Emperor Heraclius, and after centuries of oppression the Jews were granted a certain amount of freedom. Half a century later, the Caliph Abd-el-

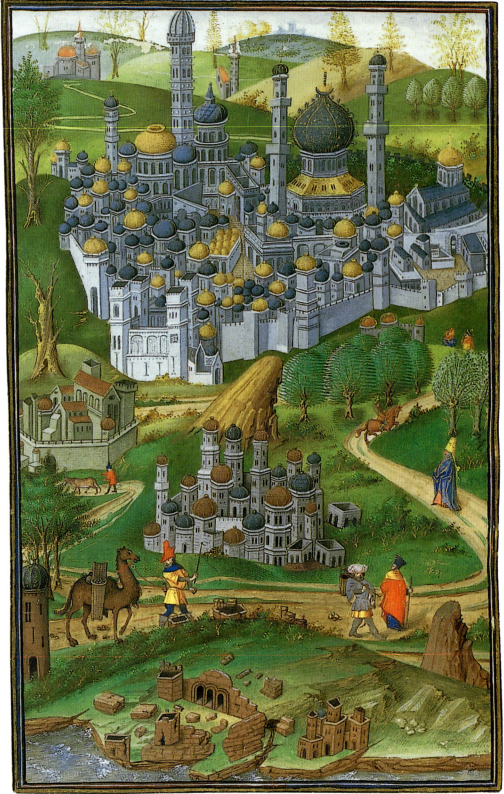

Malik visited Jerusalem and decided to build a large mosque where Solomon's temple stood because, according to tradition, it was there that Abraham built the altar to sacrifice his son Isaac and from that same place Mohammed flew toward heaven. Not far away stood the Church of the Holy Sepulcher from the time of Constantine, and this made the center of Jerusalem a sacred place for the three great monotheistic religions: Christianity, Islam and Judaism.

34 right This view of Jerusalem is a 15th-century copy taken from the Buchard manuscript of Mount Zion. Jerusalem is shown in the middle with the traditional places of pilgrimage easily identifiable: the Church of the Holy Sepulcher, Solomon's Temple, the palaces of Pilate and Herod, the Room of the Last Supper, Golgotha, the Mount of Olives and the Monastery of St. Catherine. Human figures are also shown starting their pilgrimage from Jaffa toward the Holy City.

35 This mosaic comes from the palace at Khirbet el-Mafiar, north of Jericho, known as the Palace of Isham. This building was begun during the rule of the Omayyads, the dynasty of Arab Caliphs that governed the Moslem empire from AD 661 to 750, but was never finished. The mosaic depicts pomegranate trees laden with fruit and surrounded by deer, one of which is being attacked by a lion.

36 top This 15th-century French manuscript is held in the Bibliothèque Nationale, Paris. It shows the conquest of Jerusalem in 1187 by Saladin. Saladin was Sultan of Egypt (from 1171) and of Syria (from 1174) and founder of the Ayyubid dynasty. The Christians tried unsuccessfully to retake Jerusalem in the Third Crusade (1189 – 1192), which was led by Richard I of England.

36 bottom This 15th-century French manuscript is held in the Bibliothèque Nationale, Paris. It shows the battle of St. Jean d'Acre during the Third Crusade (1189-92) when the Saracens were defeated. Leaders of this Crusade were Frederick Barbarossa, Philip II of France and Richard the Lionheart, king of England.

36-37 Between the 11th and 13th centuries, the western Christians organized Crusades to retake the Holy Land from the Moslems. There were seven main Crusades, all of which featured ferocious battles. The Crusades were preceded by an expedition of peasant followers led by Peter the Hermit in 1096, but they dispersed along the way and never reached the Holy Land.

In 1099 the Christian Crusade reached the Arab dominion of Palestine and captured Jerusalem.
The Crusaders were overthrown in 1291 by the Egyptian Mamelukes and then by the Ottoman Turks in 1516. Life in the small Jewish communities was not so different from that of the rest of the population. They all flourished in good times and suffered in times of famine or war. Invasions of locusts, earthquakes and the corruption of state employees affected everyone in the same way. Very slowly, the Jewish population started to grow again with the arrival of immigrants from Arab countries, first basing themselves in Jerusalem, Gaza, Safed and other villages in Galilee.

37 This manuscript from the middle of the 12th century shows Jerusalem (above) surrounded by walls and (below) the Crusader cavalry driving the Saracens back. Jerusalem was the site of the most brutal battles; it was always shown on medieval maps as the center of the world.

38 A Mameluke warrior on horseback grips his scimitar, the curved sword he used in battle. The Mamelukes made up a Praetorian militia in Moslem Egypt comprising Turkish and Indo-European slaves. They became the founders of two ruling dynasties in Egypt from 1250 to 1517. They managed to maintain their power after the Ottoman conquest of the country, but were defeated and then exterminated by Napoleon.

38-39 The map of Palestine drawn in 1154 by the Arab geographer Edrisi is seen here in a Persian copy made in 1533. It is oriented with south at the top, perhaps in the direction of Mecca, and is crossed diagonally by the mountains of Lebanon which divided the Mediterranean coastal region from the more important cities, marked with yellow rings.

39 This Mameluke war-axe was made with great skill by an iron-worker. The personal coat of arms of a sultan is engraved inside the half-moon blade. The lower edge of the blade is fixed to the grip so that it would not come off as a result of a downward stroke.

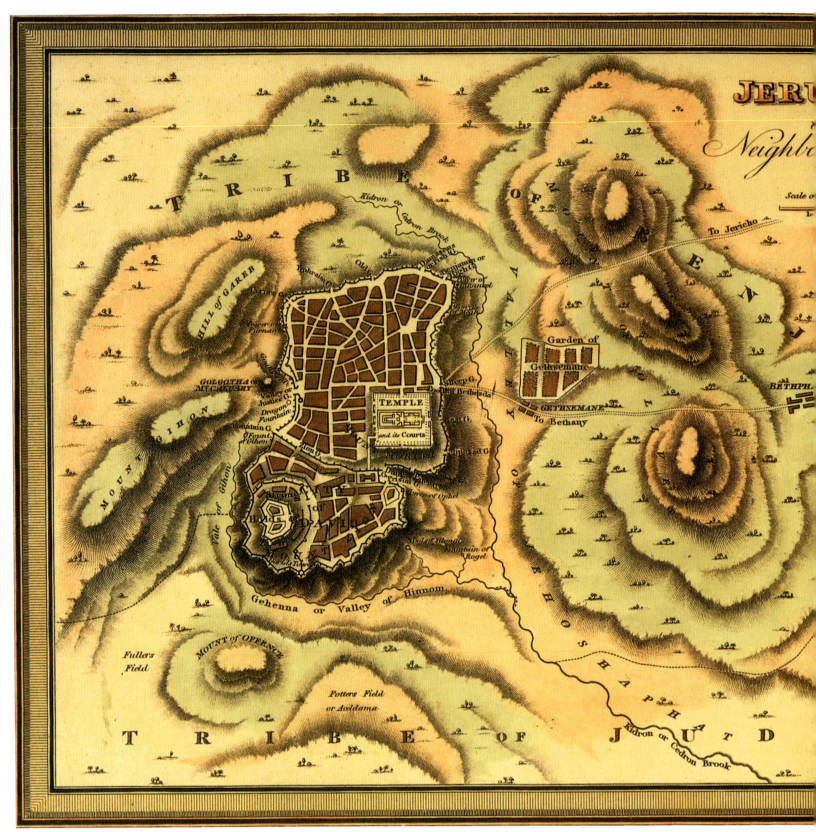

40-41 This map shows Jerusalem and its surrounding territory during the biblical era. It was printed in 1815 by an English company for the diffusion of Christianity. Mapping of the Holy Land was always especially detailed and given very careful treatment by cartographers for the particular interest this land evoked due to its importance to the three largest monotheistic religions.

40 bottom The picture shows General Kléber encouraging his men at the siege of the Crusader town of Acre in 1799, which was never taken by Napoleon. After Nelson destroyed the French fleet, Napoleon withdrew to Egypt leaving the wounded at the monastery on Mount Carmel.

41 top This oil-painting by Antoine-Jean Gros (1771-1835) shows Napoleon visiting victims of the plague in Jaffa. Napoleon attacked the Ottoman empire in Egypt despite the defeat of his fleet by Horatio Nelson (1798) at Aboukir Bay at the mouth of the Nile. Napoleon's troops were then prevented from landing at Acre in 1799 by Pasha Ahmed el-Jazzar.

During the 19th century European powers, starting with Napoleon, rediscovered the strategic and political importance of Palestine, for the presence of holy places and its position of transit between the Mediterranean and the Persian Gulf. They tried to make it a pawn in their game of alliances and rivalries with the Turkish Empire and among themselves. The most popular system to make their presence felt in the area was to open consulates in Jerusalem and to help the humanitarian organizations which assisted pilgrims. Towards the end of the century, the Jewish population grew further, particularly as a result of immigration from Russia, where anti-semitism often sparked off pogroms.

41 bottom The painter Jacques-François Joseph (1769-1823) reproduced the battle of Mount Tabor (17 February 1799) from an engraving by Louis-François Couche (1782-1823). Napoleon left his army in the Middle East to return to Paris where he overthrew the Directory and installed a military dictatorship.

In 1896 an Austrian journalist, Theodor Herzl, was struck by the antisemitism that accompanied the condemnation of Captain Dreyfus in France and he began to speak out to European Jews on the need to create a Jewish state. Between 1880 and 1910 roughly 30,000 Jews arrived in Palestine from eastern Europe. They brought with them the idea of the rebirth of the Zionist state foretold by Herzl and the collectivist spirit of socialism which they realized in farming communities founded on land bought from Turkish owners. At the outbreak of the First World War, about 100,000 Jews were living in Palestine. During the war, Palestine became one of the theaters of hostilities between Great Britain and France on one side and the Turkish empire on the other. The Jews allied themselves with the British. In 1917, as a gesture of recognition, the British Minister Arthur Balfour released a declaration in which he hoped for the creation of a "national home for the Jews" in Palestine. Strengthened by this and in spite of the hostility of the Arabs, thousands of east European Jews left for Zion after the end of the war. In 1922, the territory was entrusted to Great Britain as mandate by the League of Nations.

42 top The photograph shows the Austrian journalist Theodor Herzl (1860-1904), considered the father of Zionism. The movement was born as a response to the wave of anti-Semitism that accompanied the Dreyfus Affair in France and urged the Jews to create their own Jewish state. The first congress of the Zionist movement took place at Basel in 1897.

42 bottom Arthur J. Balfour, Conservative, is shown in this 1910 photograph. He was the British Minister for Foreign Affairs (1916-17) during the 1st World War and released a declaration in which he hoped for the creation of a "national homeland for the Jews" in Palestine. The declaration was immediately opposed by the Arabs but they were unable to stop the massive Jewish immigration into the country.

42-43 This picture taken on 9 December 1917 shows the British troops commanded by General Edmund Allenby on their entrance to Jerusalem and the handing over of the city by the Turkish authorities. In the first photograph, General Allenby is entering the city through the Jaffa Gate; in the second, Hussein Selim El-Hussein is handing over the Turkish arms to the British in the name of the Turkish authorities. In 1922, the League of Nations gave Great Britain a mandate to oversee Palestine.

43 top This 1891 picture shows a group of Russian Jews forced to flee St. Petersburg. Anti-semitism in Russia was always deep rooted and violent; pogroms, in which the local population killed Jews and destroyed their districts, made life for Jews particularly uncertain. As soon as they were able, many Jews emigrated to Palestine.

43 center and bottom The first picture shows a certificate of the National Jewish Fund issued in Germany in 1905 in which an offer is made to plant 5 olive trees; the second picture is a share of the Jewish Colonial Bank underwritten in 1900 by English Jews.

44-45
The photograph shows the British Minister for Foreign Affairs, Lord Balfour, during the inauguration in 1925 of the Jewish University in Jerusalem. This university was the second created in the Jewish state. In 1924, the Technion had already been founded in Haifa which had (and still has) only science faculties, unlike the university in Jerusalem which had (and still has) faculties for all disciplines.

44 bottom right During the British mandate over Palestine (1922-48), immigration (called "alià" or "ascent") of Jews from all around the world was especially high although the British had stipulated a maximum number of entry visas in a governmental White Paper. The first problem the new immigrant had to face, as shown in the picture, was the construction of a house to live in.

Between 1919 and 1933, above all after the rise to power of Hitler in Germany, more than 200,000 people arrived in Palestine and established many collective farms (kibbutz and moshav).
They were for the most part professionals and intellectuals and in the decades that followed they came to form the ruling class of the country. After years of curbing Arab violence against the Jews, even going to the lengths of using armoured forces and planes, the British government issued a "white paper" in 1939: this fixed narrow limits on Jewish immigration.
However, it came too late as the Jews had already created an eco-

nomic, political and administrative backbone in their state.

They had their own school and health systems, a union and two universities; they had revitalized the Jewish language, established industries and a clandestine army (the Haganah) with 60,000 men trained by officers who had originally been trained while serving in the British army. In 1940, another brigade made up of Palestinian Jews fought with the British against the Germans.

44 bottom left and 45 top The new immigrants threw themselves into agriculture and created a system of farming villages called "kibbutzim" in which members of the collective received no salary but enjoyed use of all the systems and services in the village. The first kibbutz was established at Degania in 1909. The kibbutzim system is still valid today.

45 bottom Despite the difficulties created by the British, over half a million immigrants arrived in Palestine between the two World Wars and the eve of the birth of the state of Israel. The picture shows a group of Jews on a ship heading for Palestine. The group is preparing for prayers; they have placed their phylacteries on their arms and foreheads and their prayer shawls on their shoulders.

46 top The death camp at Auschwitz was liberated by Russian troops in 1945. The Nazi death camps were responsible for the deaths of six million Jews.

46 bottom This picture shows two Jewish girls, one Polish (right) and the other Hungarian (left) with a Latvian boy in the center.

Survivors of Buchenwald concentration camp, they look out of the window of the train which flies the Israeli flag, symbol of their new-found liberty and life.

46-47 This image exemplifies illegal immigration into Palestine. During the British mandate (1922-48), a government White Paper announced a system of quotas to limit free entry to Palestine. The photograph shows some of the 7,000 refugees who arrived in Palestine on the ship President Warfield in 1947. They were transferred to British ships and taken to collection camps in Cyprus.

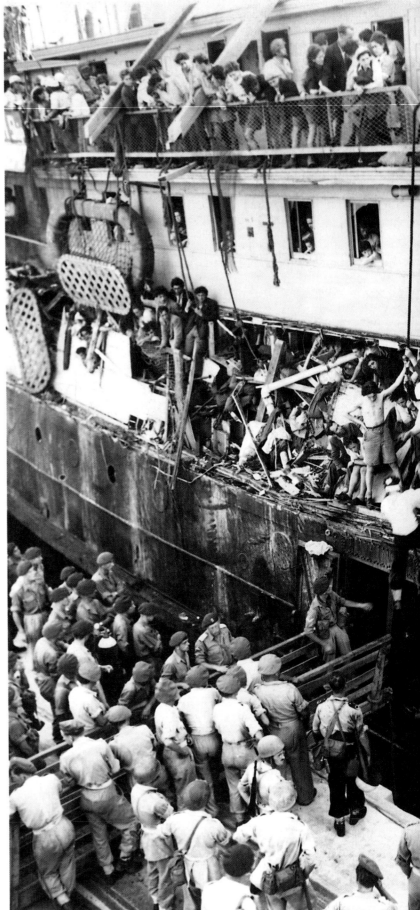

*47 top
A view of the port of Haifa in 1946 with survivors of the ship Haviva Reik which was carrying 450 refugees. After 12 dramatic days of sailing, the ship was wrecked off the coast of Haifa. Only a few managed to save themselves and reach the port. The banner in Hebrew says "Leave the doors open, we are not the last."*

47 center In the first photo, 700 refugees from central Europe are disembarking on the beaches of Nahariya.

At the end of the war, the Jews began a massive campaign for the transfer of the survivors from the German concentration camps to Palestine, but the British continued to impose the limits on immigration set by the White Paper. Nonetheless, secret organizations often managed to evade the official immigration procedures and about 85,000 Jews freed from the camps succeeded in reaching Palestine.

The "Palestine question" was brought before the United Nations in 1947, and on November 29th, with the approval of the USA and USSR, the General Assembly approved a plan for the division of the land west of the river Jordan into two states, one Jewish and one Arab, and for an international statute for the city of Jerusalem.

The plan was approved by the Jews but rejected by the countries forming the Arab League, thus sanctioning the state of war between the two communities. Meanwhile the British had said they would leave Palestine on 15 May 1948. The day before, 14 May, the committee of thirteen men which made up the de facto government of the new state of Israel, chaired by David Ben-Gurion, proclaimed its establishment.

*47 bottom
Immigration of Jews from eastern and southern Europe reached its peak in 1949 when 240,000 people arrived in Israel. Over the following years, the refugees came more from Arab countries at war with Israel.
The immigrants were immediately placed in camps as shown in this photograph of a group of huts near Jerusalem.*

48 top The British had already started to leave Israel during the early months of 1948. In the photograph a bugler salutes the British flag as it is taken down in the port of Haifa. After the official proclamation of the existence of the state of Israel on 14 May 1948, all the British left the country.

48 center Chaim Weizmann (1874-1952) was elected the first President of the state of Israel on 14 May 1948. He had already been President of the worldwide Zionist movement from 1920 to 1923 and from 1935 to 1946 and was also a famous chemist. The photograph shows his inauguration as President of the state of Israel.

48 bottom As soon as Weizmann was proclaimed President on May 14th 1948, the British troops left the country. The picture shows David Ben-Gurion with his wife as the British leave by ship. Ben-Gurion devoted all his life to the realization of the "Zionist dream" and, together with Golda Meir, was considered one of the founders of the country.

Nineteen centuries after the destruction of the temple of Solomon in Jerusalem, the Jewish state had risen again but no sooner had the British governor left the port of Haifa than the armies of Egypt, Jordan, Iraq and Syria invaded Israel. Many Arab inhabitants were forced to leave and were shut in refugee camps on the border with the promise that they would be allowed back in after the Jews were defeated.

As a matter of fact the conflict, the first of many, went in favor of the Israelis. On 15 July 1949, when the armistice was signed, the Israelis occupied a territory of over 8,000 square miles as opposed to the 6,500 assigned to them in the United Nations division plan. In addition, they controlled west Jerusalem while the old part, the eastern half, remained the territory of Jordan. In the meantime the Israelis had elected their first parliament which elected Chaim Weizmann as its first President and David Ben-Gurion as its first Prime Minister. One of the first laws that it approved was that of the "return" which gives all Jews who settle there the right to Israeli citizenship. In the following few years, in the course of which Israel became a member of the United Nations, hundreds of thousands of refugees took advantage of this offer; many of them came from Arab countries.

48-49 Immediately after the proclamation of the new Jewish state, the first Arab-Israeli war broke out. It lasted until the end of January 1949. The picture shows a road in Jerusalem, already partly in Jordanian hands, blocked by sandbags. Jerusalem was unified again only after the Six-Day War in 1967.

49 top Jewish women who had emigrated from Europe also took up arms and fought with the men on the front line to defend their country. Israeli women still do military service (only members of religious orders are exempt) and today are equal members of the Israeli army with men.

Hostilities between the Arab states and Israel never completely ceased but continued as border attacks and artillery bombardments for which Syria was mostly responsible. Syria dominated the Golan Heights from which it controlled the whole of northern Galilee.

In 1956, when Egypt nationalized the Suez Canal, a new conflict emerged within the larger one between Egypt on the one hand and Britain and France on the other. The Egyptians blocked the Strait of Tiran at the entrance to the Gulf of Eilat and the Israelis considered this an act of war. In just a few days they occupied all of Egyptian Sinai and stopped only a few miles from the Suez Canal. They withdrew only when control of the strait was taken over by soldiers from the United Nations. At this time, two people working with David Ben-Gurion in the government were Golda Meir and General Moshe Dayan without

whom the history of Israel would probably have taken a different course. Golda Meir's skills at political mediation and Moshe Dayan's strategic genius brought the country more political and military successes. However, tension continued to rise over the next ten years with terrorist attacks on settlements near to the borders and on border patrols.

At the start of June 1967, the Egyptians closed the Strait of Tiran once more after forcing the UN soldiers to leave. On June 5 the Israelis attacked the Egyptian airforce bases and defeated the Egyptian, Jordanian and Syrian forces one by one. After just six days of war, the appearance of the region had completely altered: Israel now controlled the whole of the Sinai, the Golan Heights and all of Jerusalem. Despite international pressure, the Arabs refused to open negotiations for a definitive and peaceful settlement and on 5 October 1973, the day on which the Jews celebrate the Day of Atonement, Yom Kippur, Egyptians and Syrians attacked at the same time. This time it was not easy for the Israelis to stop the enemy. They managed to do it after two weeks of bitter fighting, with the aid of international pressure which imposed a ceasefire.

50 top In this photograph of October 31th 1956 armored troops roll through Tel Aviv.

50 bottom As Chief of the General Staff in 1956, Moshé Dayan was the commanding general who defeated the Egyptians. As Minister of Defense he took to the battlefield during the Six-Day War in 1967.

50-51 The attack on Jerusalem was launched at the same time as those on Egypt, to the south, and Syria, to the north. The war lasted only six days and at the moment of the cease-fire Israel controlled the Gaza Strip, all Sinai as far as the Suez Canal, the West Bank area of Jordan and the Golan Heights to the north. Jerusalem was finally reunified.

51 bottom left Israel was once more able to consider itself united when Israeli soldiers arrived in the Temple Area.

51 top right The Golan Heights were taken by the Israelis during the Yom Kippur war, 1973.

51 top center right Moshe Dayan and Generals Barlev and Sharon study the plan of attack during the Yom Kippur War.

51 bottom center right The photograph illustrates the joy of Israeli soldiers as they cross the Golan Heights after winning them back during the Yom Kippur War.

51 bottom right Units of the Israeli fleet have occupied the Straits of Tiran after the departure of the UN soldiers.

52 top October 1978 saw the first peace agreement signed between Egypt and Israel in the presence of President Carter. The agreement was sanctioned by the Washington treaty in March 1979. Shown here is President Carter at the signing of the agreement by the Egyptian leader, Sadat, left and the Israeli Begin, on Carter's right.

The last two decades of the 20th century and the early years of the 21st have been marked by a chaotic and uncontrollable escalation in hostilities between Arabs and Israelis. However, there have also been positive signs, which have revived the same hope in both parties each time. In 1982 Israel withdrew from Sinai; in 1993 the Oslo Accords inaugurated a transitional period under the leadership of an autonomous Palestinian government; in 1994 a peace treaty with Jordan was finally signed, following almost 50 years of hostilities and in 2000 Israel withdrew from southern Lebanon, which it had occupied since 1982. In a less extreme situation, each of these episodes alone would have sufficed to ensure peace. However, here this was not the case. Between 2000 and 2005 all efforts were frustrated by periodic outbreaks of violence from both factions. On the other hand, in 2003 bilateral negotiations between Israel and Syria, an unbend-

52 center Public order in the administered Territories slowly but continuously degenerated after 1987. The Arabs started the "intifadam" attacking the Israeli troops with stones, in an attempt to gain greater independence in the lands where they lived, administered by the Israelis. The photograph shows a demonstrator in the streets of Ramallah in 1988.

52 bottom As guests of President Clinton, Yitzhak Rabin and Yasser Arafat shook hands for the first time in front of the whole world on 13 September 1993, in Washington. Following this meeting, the Palestinians took over direct administration of some of the territories they lived in, one of which was the Gaza Strip.

53 top On 10 December 1994, Yasser Arafat (President of the PLO), Shimon Peres (Israeli Minister for Foreign Affairs) and Yitzhak Rabin (Prime Minister of Israel) received the Nobel Peace Prize in Stockholm in recognition of their work in advancing the rapprochement between the Israelis and the Palestinians.

ing supporter of the Palestinian State, gradually allowed the definition of two sovereign states: an Israel without external threats and a democratic Palestine. Furthermore, the death in 2004 of Yasser Arafat, Chairman of the Palestine Liberation Organization, opened up new horizons with the election of Mahmoud Abbas as the movement's new leader. In 2005 two episodes confirmed the genuine intention of both parties to achieve peace; firstly the Sharm el-Sheikh agreement attempted to contain the violence, and shortly afterwards the Israeli army withdrew from the Gaza Strip, which it had occupied since 1967. In 2007 the contradictory evolution of Palestinian internal politics, which has lead to a sort of civil war between the factions of Fatah and Hamas, rekindled the doubts of those who still consider peace a long way off. However, it is the only possible prospect for a country that has already experienced too many conflicts.

53 bottom The assassination of Yitzhak Rabin in 1995 by an Israeli extremist during a demonstration of supporters of the peace process threw the country into depression. It seemed as though the rapprochement between the two peoples had come to a halt once and for all. Many heads of state were present at his funeral, including King Hussein of Jordan.

THE PLACES WHERE THE PAST IS WRITTEN

54 bottom The Palace of Hisham in Jericho was the residence of the Omayyads, the first successors to Mohammed. The building was begun by Caliph Hisham (724-743) and continued by his successor el-Walid.

54-55 Jericho is thought to be the oldest city in the world. It was built on the Tel es-Sultan hill between the springhead of the Elisha and the modern city in the middle of the Judaean desert.

55 top left The community at Qumran lived on a rocky spur overlooking the Dead Sea. The aridity of the desert and the difficulty of access were natural defenses. Some consider that Qumran was a caravan station for travellers on the "salt road" from Jerusalem to Arabia.

55 top right This elegant decoration in sandstone has been rebuilt in the courtyard of the Palace of Hisham in Jericho. The entrance hall gives way to a square internal courtyard where a covered water basin stood. The palace was destroyed by an earthquake prior to completion.

54 top The Dead Sea Scrolls were enclosed in clay amphoras and hidden in caves. The scrolls were hidden near Qumran by inhabitants of the village in AD 68-70.

The history of Israel can be read in the rocks and stones of its countryside. In the green plains of the north or on the Mediterranean coast, in the desert of Judaea, around the Dead Sea and in the craters of the Negev the past can always be read under the sun whether it relates to biblical history or the Gospel, the struggles against the Assyrians and the Romans, or the lives of the medieval hermits.

There is one region where this imaginary history book opens its most fascinating and mysterious pages. It is the area that runs along the Dead Sea from Jericho, to the north, to Masada, to the south. Its heart is the desert of Judaea. Whoever visits it is forever struck by its unique contrast: on the one hand, nature, that has attacked the land for millions of years as though wanting to demonstrate just how violent it can be; on the other, man, who has lived there for thousands of years and left signs of his passing everywhere. Traveling just a few miles south from Jericho to the extreme north of the Dead Sea is like traveling through ten thousand years of history.

The ruins of the oldest city in the world have not left signs of Joshua's assault but what can be read of man's past more than sufficiently compensates for this lack. Jericho is situated nine hundred feet below sea-level, the lowest inhabited point in the world. It was here that man first discarded his hunting origins to become a member of a farming community. He had not yet learnt about pottery, his priority being to surround the settlement with strong fortifications. Conquered, destroyed, rebuilt and fortified again by unknown peoples, Amorites, Canaanites and Hebrews, passed between the hands of Babylonians, Assyrians, Cleopatra and others up to the times of Herod the Great, Jericho is much more evidence of man's ability to recreate his civilization than to destroy it.

A little south of Jericho lies Qumran, almost on the shore of the Dead Sea. It is no more than a spur of rock sticking out into the great salt lake perforated by caves and a few remains of a human settlement, but Qumran's value is incommensurable for man. After the Second World War, clay jars were found in its caves that contained thousands of manuscripts in scrolls and fragments written over a period of about two hundred years, from 150 BC to AD 68, by Essenes, a community of Hebrew monks.

The manuscripts, known as the Dead Sea Scrolls, are now housed in the Book Sanctuary in Jerusalem's National Museum of Israel. They contain lots of information on the life of the monastic community but above all they are religious documents and contain commentaries on sacred texts among which is almost the whole of the biblical book of the prophet Isaiah. Studies have shown that few differences exist between this text and the version that has been handed down to us as part of the Bible. This means that the Jewish Bible has changed little since the times of Jesus.

55

56 top left The fort of Masada stands on an isolated outcrop surrounded by hills in the desert on the western bank of the Dead Sea.

56 top right Herod the Great's palace-cum-fortress at Masada had internal walls decorated with frescoes in floral and geometric patterns, some of which still remain.

56-57 The fort is protected on all sides by steep drops. Zealots and Essenes sheltered here from the Romans in AD 73. When it became clear to them that they could not repulse the siege of the Roman army, they committed mass suicide. The ramp built by the Romans to reach the fort can be seen on the right.

57 top left The picture shows the columns of the heating system which held up the floor of the calidarium of the largest baths.

57 top right The northern palace was built as a personal residence for King Herod. The colonnaded circular rooms on the highest and

Even further south, where the Dead Sea is at its narrowest and the coast of Jordan seems almost within reach, there is Masada. Masada represents some of the most important events in the history of this land and introduces us to one of its most controversial figures, Herod the Great. Herod was an able politician, a great builder and a loyal friend to Rome but it seems that Augustus, the Roman emperor, said "I would rather be one of Herod's pigs than one of his sons."

The area is on a plateau 1,600 feet high above the shore of the Dead Sea. The top is oval, about 20 acres in size, stretching from north to south. Such a place can be used only as a fortress and its Jewish name *metzuda* means just that. The first to use it for that purpose were the Maccabees (2nd century BC) but the first person to render it impregnable was Herod. A barracks, however, was not welcoming enough for him so he turned it into a palace.

Herod hid there in 42 BC when the Parthians conquered Jerusalem. Using an army of slaves, in only six years he built a masterpiece which was also able to protect him from other dangers: first of all by his own people who hated him, and then from Cleopatra of Egypt. Herod encircled the plateau with a double wall and towers at regular intervals. Inside were barracks, stores, accommodation for the staff, and water tanks, canals and aqueducts. Men and donkeys were used to carry the water from the lowest to the highest tanks. There were also two palaces: the western one, used for official occasions, had a throne room and an apartment with hot and cold water. The other palace, on the northern tip of the plateau, was the everyday palace. To complete it were three more buildings on top of one another on the sides of the mountain, each with large colonnaded terraces from which to admire the view of the Dead Sea.

Ironically, after the destruction of the temple in Jerusalem by Titus in AD 70, the fortress fell into the hands of the zealots who had started the great revolt against Rome. They found the fortress so well stocked with food and arms that they were able to hold out against the Romans for three years. The task of taking the fortress fell to general Flavius Silva and the Tenth Legion. Each assault proved useless until the Romans took a drastic decision: to build an earthen rampart, still almost entirely intact, to reach the walls of Masada. When the zealots realized there was no defence against the Romans, ten people were picked to kill the others and then themselves. Only five children and two women survived the massacre, from whom the historian Josephus later took down an account of what had happened.

When they reached the fortress, the Romans found 960 bodies and large reserves of food which the zealots had left to show that they had not killed themselves for fear of starvation. Today Masada is a destination of pilgrimage for thousands of Israelis, a sacred place where the visitors promise that "Masada will not fall a second time" and that the Jews will never again be slaves.

second highest floors were for receiving important guests. The rectangular third floor had small baths in Roman style.

57 bottom right The floors inside the palace-cum-fortress are enriched with mosaics. The palace was built for social purposes and as a means of celebrating Herod's power and wealth.

*58 top left
Beersheba stands on a flat land at the edge of the Negev Desert. The place is mentioned in the Bible because it was here that Abraham dug a well in the presence of King Abimelech.*

Abraham gave the king seven lambs in return for agreeing to an alliance. The biblical name Beersheba is interpreted as meaning "the well of seven" or "well of the oath."

58 top right The mosaic floor in the synagogue of En Gedi on the Dead Sea dates from the 5th century AD. The Bible describes En Gedi as a city of vines and palms. Its wealth depended on its abundant supply of water.

*58-59
The Herodium fortress is one of the most architecturally unusual structures in the western world. It dominates the barren range of Judaean semi-desert hills. The palace was built by Herod the Great on the top of a semi-artificial hill with a tank at its base used to store water and for bathing.*

In 2007 a group of archeologists from the Hebrew University discovered the tomb of Herod the Great in one of the rooms atop the Herodium. Although he was buried wearing a gold crown and holding a scepter, the royal emblems have never been found, and only fragments were discovered in the eight-foot-long (2.5 m) sarcophagus.

59 top The Church of the Nativity stands in the center of Bethlehem. It was built around 540 during the time of Emperor Justinian. The account given by Eusebius, the Palestinian bishop of Caesarea and the biographer of Emperor Constantine, says that the first construction here was a church built by Constantine in 326 on the site of an ancient holy cave.

59 center The cave of the Nativity may be seen in the church of the same name in Bethlehem. It is rectangular, 40 feet long and 10 feet high. The altar that celebrates the birth of Christ, to the left, is administered by Greek Orthodox monks; the altars of the Manger and the Wise Men, to the right, are administered by the Franciscans.

59 bottom A silver star on a slab of marble inside the Church of the Nativity in Bethlehem marks the spot where Jesus was born. Around it there is the inscription, "Here Jesus Christ was born of the Virgin Mary". The fifteen lamps that shine on the star represent the different Christian creeds.

Another of Herod's masterpieces is situated a few miles south of Bethlehem. It is the Herodium (or Herodion), the fortress palace and final resting place of the king, as demonstrated by a team of researchers in 2007. Indeed, one of its rooms was found to house the remains of a royal sarcophagus that archeologists have attributed with certainty to Herod. As a fortress the Herodium is unique. It stands on the round summit of a hill which Herod had encircled by two walls with a diameter of 220 feet and four towers, each 100 feet high, so that the complex had the form of a cloverleaf. Much of the fortress was built out of the heart of the hill and, like Masada, everything necessary for a life of luxury was provided: baths, water tanks, mosaic floors, large stores of food, etc. Lower inside the hill there was a maze of tunnels to allow exit without being seen. This fortress too was used in a revolt against the Romans: in AD 135 men, women and children took refuge here in a final attempt at resistance. General Lucilius Bassus forced them to surrender by lighting fires at the entrances to the tunnels so making the air inside the fort unbreathable. The places where the ancient history of Israel was created are very numerous and scattered. The Bible speaks of the Promised Land as stretching from the river Dan in northern Galilee to Beersheba at the start of the Negev. Right next to the Dan, archeologists have found a settlement that has been dated to the times of the Twelve Tribes and which is one of the oldest and best preserved sites in the country.

60 top left The ruins of the ancient Roman theater of Ashkelon, a city-port to the south of Tel Aviv, are preserved in a national park. Herod the Great was born in Ashkelon, which became a cultural center during the Byzantines era. Many of its archaeological remains are from the 4th century, when the area was under Roman rule, but Crusader remains are also to be seen.

60 center left Important catacombs in Bet She'arim in Galilee are indicative of customs and traditions of the Jews in the 2nd century AD. After the destruction of Solomon's Temple in AD 70, some Jews hid in this area where they built a necropolis in the soft rock of the hills.

60 top right Excavations at Hazor in upper Galilee were carried out systematically from 1956 to 1958 and from 1968 to 1970 by Yigael Yadin of the Jewish University of Jerusalem. His work shows that Hazor was divided into two distinct parts: an upper city on the hilltop covering 5 acres and a lower city covering 175 acres at the foot of the hill.

60 center right The famous Phoenician porto Dor lies behind the remains of a Roman theater and a church. The site near Haifa is mentioned for the first time in an ancient Egyptian inscription from the 13th century BC, in the reign of Ramesses II. Archaeologists proved that it was inhabited from the 12th century BC by Canaanites and Phoenicians.

60 bottom right This fine limestone head found in Dor represents the goddess of fortune, Tiche, recognizable by her crown. She was venerated as the protectress of towns and villages.

61 Megiddo stood on an important caravan route, the Via Maris. Archaeological remains found here can be dated back to 3300 BC and it is evident that the settlement was originally a religious center. The sacred area with a circular platform and three temples was used for more than 2,000 years. The large grain silo was built during the time of the Divided Monarchy.

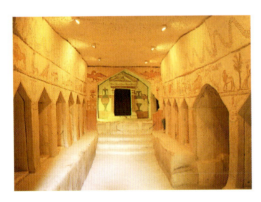

Still in the north, on the slopes of Mount Carmel that overlooks the modern city of Haifa on the Mediterranean, archaeologists have found the remains of a port four thousand years old, the port of Dor. It was first used by the Phoenicians who built a fort there and used the port as a jumping-off point for trading voyages throughout the Mediterranean. The port was also used by the Egyptians, Canaanites, Babylonians, Persians, Greeks and the Crusaders. Its natural bay once offered refuge to the ships of Napoleon Bonaparte in 1799 (long after the port had been destroyed) after the defeat at Acre, now named Akko.

The city of David in Jerusalem, with its terraces, tunnels, canals and swimming pools is the most important, but not unique, example of ancient Jewish town design in the Hebrew kingdoms two thousand years before Christ. The magnificence of this civilization has been brought to public attention with the excavation of the hill at Megiddo near Nazareth where, starting in 1903, twenty successive layers of civilization were found, starting with the Iron Age and reaching up to the Greek Empire, when the large city-fortress of Megiddo was reduced to a village.

60 bottom left The caves at Bet Guvrin near Latrun were discovered in 1962. These stone caves were used between the 4th and the 7th century, then turned into tombs and later chapels (as shown by the crosses sculpted out of the walls). The most interesting tomb is decorated with pictures of animals including Cerberus, the three-headed dog.

62 top left The photograph shows columns with Ionic capitals from the "road with shops" from the Roman city of Bet She'an, one of Israel's oldest sites. The first settlements found here date back to the 5th millennium BC.

62 bottom left The archaeological area of Hammat Gader overlooks the valley of the river Yarmuk near Lake Tiberias. The remains stand inside a park with modern bathing facilities. During the Roman era, Hammat Gader was part of the decapolis that existed up to the end of the 2nd century. Excavations have uncovered a theater and baths from Roman times and a 5th-century synagogue.

62 right This basalt stela from the late Bronze Age was found during excavations at Bet She'an. At that time the city was in the hands of the Egyptians. The upper panel shows two lions ready to fight; the lower panel pictures a dog attacking a lion. The perimeters of several houses in the city were surrounded by such stones.

62-63 Bet She'an is one of Israel's oldest sites with its earliest remains dating from the 5th millennium BC. During early Roman times the main part of the settlement was at the foot of the hill. The Roman theater dug out from the slopes of the hill is one of the best preserved in Israel. It is 260 feet in diameter and made from black basalt.

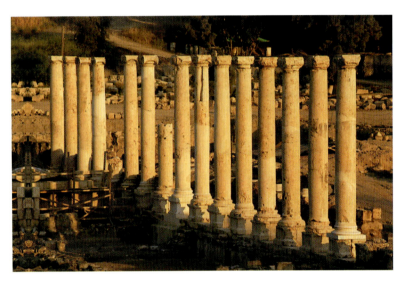

During the long period of Roman domination, the Jews built many of their most interesting synagogues such as those at Baram, Korazim, Gamla, Kurzi and Kapharnoum, center of the apostolic life of Jesus in Galilee. The Romans too left traces of their passage at Caesarea, Bet She'an, along the Jordan valley, Banyas, at the source of that river, in Jerusalem of course, and at Sepphoris where beautiful mosaics were found, one of which is called the "Mona Lisa of Galilee." The archaeological remains left by the Romans give us an idea of the size and the power the Roman Empire attained. On top of the Roman remains traces have been found of the successor Byzantine civilization, though without damage to the former.

63 top left Remains of a synagogue at Kapharnoum in Galilee stand next to a modern octagonal building that covers the remains of a Byzantine church which, according to tradition, was built over the site of Peter's house. Much of the life of Jesus was spent in this area. Peter and Andrew, the disciples of Jesus, lived in Kapharnoum.

63 top right The synagogue of Qazrin on the Golan Heights was built between the 3rd and 4th century, then rebuilt in the 5th century and discovered in 1972 during restoration work. It was built from blocks of basalt and divided into three naves with two rows of columns. One of the door jambs is decorated with a three-armed menorah and a peacock. The building was destroyed by an earthquake in 746.

64 top left and top right The mosaic known as the "Mona Lisa of Galilee" can be seen in the 1st-century palace of Sepphoris. The Mona Lisa is part of a mosaic based on a Dionysian theme covering the whole living room and divided into scenes of Greek life. The palace was destroyed by an earthquake in 363 following which the whole area was abandoned.

64 center left, bottom left and 65 Interesting archaeological findings in Tiberias on the western shore of the lake of the same name are held in the Hammat Tiberias national park. A 4th-century mosaic covers the floor of the synagogue. The central panel depicts the four seasons with the twelve signs of the zodiac named in Hebrew.

64 bottom right At Bet She'an, not far from Tiberias, mosaics of great beauty have been found such as the one depicting the zodiac on the floor of the 6th-century BC synagogue at Bet Alpha. This mosaic uses extremely vivid colours based on tones of yellow, orange, green and blue. The upper part of the Hammat Tiberias mosaic shows the Ark of the Covenant containing the Ten Commandments. This is flanked by two lit seven-branched lamps and other ritual objects.

66 top The archaeological area of Caesarea stretches for almost two miles beside the sea, from the last section of the aqueduct in the north to the Roman theater in the south. The port area and Crusader citadel are situated in the middle. The picture shows the ruins of what is believed to be Herod's palace with the large central tank half-submerged in the sea.

66 bottom There is much archaeological evidence of the Crusaders period at Caesarea, like this building with its pointed vaults in the photograph. Caesarea was a busy and important city in Roman times; the Byzantine emperor Heraclius conquered it in 627 but in 640 it passed into Arab hands and fell into ruin. In 1099 the Crusaders arrived and it flourished once more as a port.

66-67 The water supply system created by Herod the Great at Caesarea used two aqueducts. The main aqueduct was over 5 miles long and carried water from the Carmel springs north of the city. The ruins of this engineering triumph still cross the countryside north of Caesarea, alongside the extensive sandy beach.

67 top left The walls that still enclose the old city of Acre (today Akko) were built on Crusader foundations during two subsequent periods in history. In 1749, Daher el-Omar built the first ring which withstood the Napoleonic siege and, from 1799, el-Jazzar began their reconstruction which was completed by his successors. In the 19th century, they suffered great damage.

67 top right Some of the most important Crusader buildings in Acre were found under what was a government hospital. The refectory of the Order of St. John dates from c. 1148. During the Ottoman era it was filled with earth and stones up to the upper level of the stone columns which held up the vault, so that more support would be given to the new buildings above.

68 top The Crusader castle of Belvoir was built in the Jordan valley from the black basalt rock found there. In the photograph it is possible to recognize one of the slits in the keep. The inner keep is the castle's last line of defense. If the external walls were breached, the defenders were able to retire into the barbican or the large donjon.

68 center The Crusader castle of Monfort was built in 1226 by the Knights of the Teutonic Order at a height of 600 feet in the valley of Nahal Keziv so that it looked like "the prow of a gigantic ship entering the green hills of Galilee." It was the Order's general headquarters, where the archives and treasures where kept and where the soldiers rested after battle.

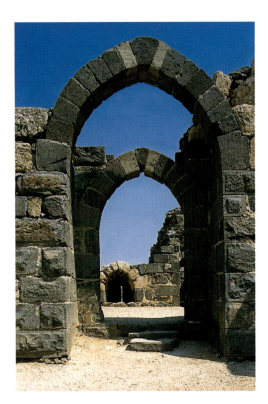

Much evidence of the era of the Crusades remains, particularly at Jerusalem and Acre (Akko), but there are also Crusader castles to be found in Galilee and the Jordan valley. Here the castle of Belvoir (or the Star of Jordan) was built completely in black basalt 1,500 feet above the river in a position that looks over from Samaria to Galilee as far as the mountains of Jordan. At the time it seemed impregnable but when Saladin the Turk thought of destroying the foundations of the external keep, it was the end. The Turks were able to enter the castle and destroy it completely.

68 bottom The fortress of Yehi'am was built in upper Galilee during the 12th century by the Order of Templars. It was destroyed in 1265 by the Mameluke Sheikh Baibars. The thick walls enclosed a courtyard onto which large two-story buildings opened. The fortress was partially rebuilt in the middle of the 19th century by Daher el-Omar and it was used in the war of 1948.

68-69 Nimrud castle on the Golan Heights is the largest of the Crusader castles in Israel. The legend says that it was built by the biblical hero Nimrod, king of Babylon and founder of Nineveh. Owned by the Arabs, the castle was occupied and rebuilt by the Crusaders in 1129 to protect Banyas from the Arabs. It was dismantled during the Fifth Crusade.

69 top Belvoir Castle is known as the "Star of Jordan." It was founded as a fortified farm in 1140 and sold to the Order of the Hospitallers in 1168. It resisted the assaults of Saladin on two occasions, in 1182 and 1183, but a month after victory at the battle of the Horns of Hattin in 1187, Saladin captured Belvoir. The castle was destroyed in 1217-18.

70 left and top right Abda is the modern name for the ancient city of Obada which is now a national park. Abda was situated on a crossroads of major trading routes. It was also important as a civil and religious center as shown by the remains of a 5th-century Byzantine church. The city was destroyed in 614 by the Persians and occupied by the Moslems soon after.

70 bottom right The small bronze panther from the 1st century BC was found during excavations at Abda and can now be seen in the Israel Museum, in Jerusalem. The Nabatean city of Abda flourished during the Byzantine era thanks to frequent pilgrimages to the Sinai. The city began to lose its importance from the time of the Moslem conquest and was eventually abandoned.

70-71 The Nabateans were a nomadic people that traded throughout the desert. They created three stopping points on their caravan routes in the Negev Desert where they employed ingenious systems for conserving water: Abda, Mamshit and Shivta. Shivta is the modern name for Subeita, which became a large city during Byzantine rule when the nomadic Nabateans were forced to remain in one place.

71 top left The desert sand that covered some Nabatean cities also preserved many old buildings. The aerial photograph shows the site of Mamshit which was a prosperous trading centre in the Byzantine era.

71 top right The main ruins at Shivta are of three Byzantine churches. The southerly church has three naves, wall frescoes and geometric pattern mosaics on the floor. The central church is the most recent of the three; it has a baptism font in the shape of a cross. The northerly church is dedicated to St. George and has mosaic flooring.

Equally interesting are the remains of Hazor in northern Galilee near the Arab city of Ramla, and of Timma near Eilat, where King Solomon had his copper mines.

The spice road of the semi-nomadic trading people from the Arabian peninsula, the Nabateans, passed through the Negev. The Nabateans travelled up the Red Sea during the 3rd century BC leaving traces of their progress. The spice road started in Petra in Jordan and reached the Mediterranean by passing across the southern deserts of Israel. The archaeological remains of the cities of Shivta, Mamshit and Avdat have shown of water collection and conservation techniques the Nabateans used to irrigate their crops. These techniques that have been adapted for modern desert colonies, and which are successful.

72 top left
The Greek Orthodox monastery of Quarentena stands on the north-western mountains overlooking the plain of Jericho. This is one of the monasteries in the Judaean desert where Jesus was supposed to have first been tempted by the Devil. It was built at the end of the last century.

72 center left and bottom left Near to the monastery of Mar Saba stands the chapel of St. Nicholas. Inside there are five 15th-century icons and, in a room facing the entrance, the reliquaries of monks martyred by Persians and Arabs. Close by in the church of Theotokos lies the tomb of St. Saba whose body was brought from Venice whence it had been taken by the Crusaders.

72 top right Nebi Musa is situated in the valley of Kidron not far from the Herodium in the Judaean desert. Popular Moslem tradition tells us that Moses is buried here, but as to the tomb "nobody knows where it may be." Nebi Musa boasts a large mosque whose white domes can be seen from far off.

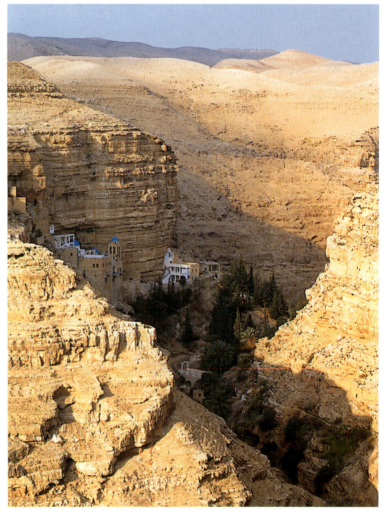

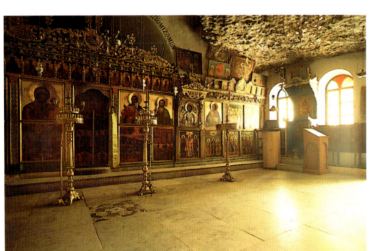

72 bottom right The monastery of St. George of Koziba in the desert of Judaea is the oldest known shrine to the Virgin. The first hermits gathered in caves here in 420-430 and transformed one into a chapel dedicated to St. Stephen Protomartyr.

73 The monastery of Mar Saba, south east of Jerusalem, looks over the narrow Kidron valley. It was founded in 483 by St. Saba, a monk who was born in Cappadocia (439-532) and who lived in the hermitage from the age of five. In the 6th and 7th centuries the monastery welcomed important visitors such as John of Damascus and Stephen Thaumaturge. Women were, and still are, excluded.

A SMALL LAND OF A THOUSAND COLORS

*74 left
The Mediterranean coastline gets higher as one goes north until it becomes spectacular at Rosh Haniqra on the Lebanese border.*

74 top right On the coast north of Haifa between Nahariyya and Rosh Haniqra, Achziv national park has been created, famous for its beautiful beaches. These look onto a group of islets which are also a nature reserve.

74 bottom right A wide sandy beach closed off by dunes runs along much of the Mediterranean coast of the country. Beaches within and outside the cities are crowded with tourists in search of sun and fresh air all year round, not to mention Israelis who like an outdoor life.

74-75 At Ashkelon-Zikim on the Mediterranean coast south-west of Tel Aviv, there is a long stretch of protected sandy coast which is ideal for discovering the life that abounds in the dune habitat that at first glance seems arid and uninhabited.

75 top left Carmel is a range of mountains roughly 1,550 feet high that stretches for 15 miles south of Haifa. It is a protected area made up of small nature reserves containing prehistoric caves and archaeological remains.

75 top right Israel's water resources comprise the river Jordan, Lake Tiberias and several small river systems.

In an area just about the size of Wales, one that can be crossed north-south by car in about eight hours and east-west in only two, Israel presents an extreme variety of landscapes: a long flat coastline, chains of mountains, a desert that covers two-thirds of the country and a wide valley through which the river Jordan runs to reach the Dead Sea, the largest depression in the world. And yet the Jews who returned to the Land of the Fathers a hundred years ago found an environment that had been impoverished by nature much as the rest of the Middle East had. Where in the past there had been forests and extensive fertile agricultural land, now there was stony ground, meager pastures and scrubby fields on the valley bottoms only. The mountain sides had been washed away and left arid, the flatlands were covered with marshes or sand dunes.

In a century the face of the country has been changed. Colonists reclaimed the entire central coastal area and created more than 326,000 acres of forests, chiefly pine and eucalyptus. They also established dozens of national parks and nature reserves (an astonishing number considering the size of the territory), reintroducing plants and animals that thrived during the biblical era but later disappeared. All inhabitants have been taught to participate in the rebirth of nature in their country. Children are encouraged to plant a tree on every celebration or in memory of someone, to respect the flowers which grow on roadside borders, and told not to cut down even a single tree. A bird's eye view of the country travelling from north to south would give a clear idea of how in a small surface area can exist uncontaminated places, not far from urbanized areas or deserts.

From the Lebanese border right down to Gaza, where Israel and Egypt meet, the coast is a sandy strip bordered by heavily farmed areas which extend up to twenty-eight miles inland at some points. This sandy strip was no more than a large dune area at the beginning of the century but now is the most heavily populated part of Israel. The main cities, ports and most heavy industry is found here; Tel Aviv represents the centre of a large connurbation that stretches from Netanya to the north as far as Ashkelon to the south.

In the extreme north of the country,

76 top The Jordan runs into and out of Lake Tiberias. After running through an embanked section, it enters the lake from the north, then meanders south as shown in the photograph on the left. The waters of Lake Tiberias and the Jordan are filled with religious significance for Christians who come to be baptized.

76-77 The basalt Golan Heights dominate the long valley of Hula along which the river Jordan runs. All Golan, Syrian up till 1967, is poorly inhabited although there are a few Druse villages like that of Majdal Shams, in the photograph, or the one near Masada where shops selling local handcrafts can be found.

77 top Mount Hermon, at 8,667 feet, is snow-covered for many months of the year. It is the only mountain in Israel that receives snow, so has been equipped for winter sports with ski-lifts and tourist facilities. The proximity of these pistes to the warmth of the beaches is appreciated by tourists.

77 center The springs of the Banjas are one of the largest natural attractions in the Golan national park. Among its luxuriant vegetation and Roman ruins, the park contains the remains of the Grotto of Pan, the Greek god to which the city called "Panaeas" was dedicated. The Banjas forms the river Jordan after the confluence with the Dan and the Hashani.

77 bottom The Jordan is formed by the confluence of three tributaries, the Hashani, the Dan and the Banjas which merge soon after their source on Mount Hermon. From the rising to its outlet in the Dead Sea, the Jordan is 155 miles long although its many twists and turns make its actual passage 206 miles long.

in northern Galilee, the countryside starts to differ. The Golan Heights were formed by volcanic eruptions and are now steep mountains that dominate the valley of Hula; Mount Hermon, where the river Jordan has its source, is 9,000 feet high. This is the high Jordan valley which used to be wholly covered in marshland, difficult to cultivate and infested with malaria until a few decades ago. When the valley was dried out, it provided 20,000 acres of fertile farmland and a large quantity of precious water which used to be lost in the swamps. Recently, to recover some of the area's natural characteristics, a small part of the valley was flooded once more and a nature reserve was created where now wild boar, mongeese, jungle cats, buffalo and coypu live. Twice a year, in March and October, hundreds of thousands of birds have started to pass over the valley again on their migrations from Africa to Asia and eastern Europe and vice versa.

78 top left The Ginnosar kibbutz was founded in 1937 on the shore of Lake Tiberias. It is famous for its Yigal Allon center which contains a fishing boat dating from the period 1st century BC – 1st century AD. The boat appeared in the lake during a drought in 1985.

78 bottom left During the Byzantine era, a fisherman's house found at Kapharnoum on Lake Tiberias was identified as the house of St. Peter. An octagonal Greek Orthodox church was built (see photograph) to preserve what remained of the house. As a center of Jesus' activities, Kapharnoum is sacred to Christians today.

The Hula valley is the first tract of the gigantic Asian-African tectonic split that becomes the Great Rift Valley in Africa. It runs the length of Israel into the Lake Tiberias (650 feet below sea level), continues as the Jordan valley between the mountains of Judaea and Samaria to the west and Gilead and Moab in Jordan to the east, passes by the Dead Sea (1,250 feet below sea level, the deepest depression in the world) and the Aravà savannah as far as Eilat on the Red Sea. It then continues to Africa along the Dancala Depression to reach the region of the great lakes. Lake Tiberias is the main fresh-water reserve in Israel. It is seven miles wide, thirteen miles long and 160 feet deep. There are important archaeological and religious sites on its shores that have particular reference to Christian times as the area was very closely linked with the life of Jesus. There are, of course, towns like Tiberias around it and tourist resorts, spas and farming villages.

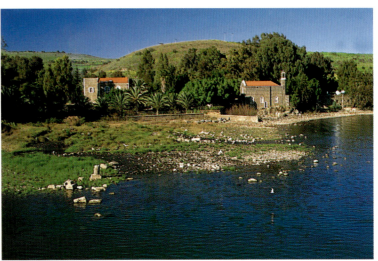

78 top right The present Church of the Miracle of the Loaves and the Fishes was built at Tabgha where previous shrines had stood: the first was built in 352 BC and a second, covered in mosaics, in AD 450. The second building was destroyed in 614 and forgotten until 1932. The mosaics were then discovered, like the one showing the miracle of the loaves and the fishes.

78 center right The city of Tabgha stands on the Via Maris on the north-west shore of Lake Tiberias at the foot of the Mount of the Beatitudes. Christian tradition tells us that three episodes from the Gospels took place here, each celebrated in its own sanctuary: the miracle of the oares and fishes, the Sermon on the Mount and the miracle of Peter's fishing catch.

78 bottom right and 79 Lake Tiberias is also called the Sea of Galilee or Kinneret and is the largest freshwater reserve in Israel. It measures 13 miles by 7 and has an average depth of 157 feet. The lake fills a depression at 695 feet below sea level and is filled with fish. It is also a religious tourist destination as episodes from the lives of Jesus and Peter took place here.

80 top and 81 top right As Israel is perennially short of water reserves, all that it receives is such a precious asset that it is obliged to channel every single drop, including rainwater. The national aqueduct, completed in 1964, has a grid of conduits, reserves and pumping stations that carry water from northern regions to the center and the semi-arid south.

80 center Nazareth is halfway between the Mediterranean and Lake Tiberias and stands on the foothills of the mountains of Galilee. It is the largest Arab city in Israel and has a modern, chaotic part and an old one that has maintained the typical narrow streets. With Jerusalem and Bethlehem, the city is one of the most important centers for Christians.

80 bottom The Jordan valley, in the photograph, is the zone where agricultural specialization in Israel has reached its zenith. Use of agricultural machinery and electronic equipment designed and produced in the country has meant a reduction in costs, an increase in yields, an improvement of quality and labour savings.

80-81 The existing Basilica of the Transfiguration was built on Mount Tabor in Galilee in 1924 by the architect Barluzzi. The basilica has three naves and, under the apse, a crypt which commemorates Jesus' transfiguration. The altar is the original one found during excavations; traces of a previous Crusader church can also be seen.

81 top left The moshav of Nahalal is in Galilee, in the valley of Jezreel, also known simply as "the valley." The design reflects the spokes of a wheel and is an experiment based on irrigated crops. As with all agricultural cooperatives of this type, buildings and services are common property while the fields are cultivated individually.

Galilee covers all of northern Israel. It is a region of gentle, rounded hills, all terraced. The highest one is Mount Meron at 3,100 feet and at its foot stands Safed, the city that became the center of Jewish mysticism and the Kabbala in the 16th century. It is still known today as a center of Talmudic studies and for its large presence of artists from all around the world, attracted by its mystical atmosphere. Galilee ends at the valley of Jezreel which for Israelis is "the valley." It divides the mountains of Galilee on the northern side from those of Judaea and Samaria on the south. From the top of Mount Tabor (only 1,800 feet high) it is possible to look over the whole of the valley and see the fields cultivated by cooperative farming communities (kibbutz and moshav), large Arab villages and small towns as well as Nazareth (so important to Christians) and archaeological areas from the biblical and even prehistoric eras such as Megiddo and Bet She'an.

82 The nature reserve of En Gedi covers 66 square miles along the shore of the Dead Sea. At its center is a spectacular spring called En David, a luxuriant subtropical vegetation and a rich wildlife. The reserve also contains prehistoric and archaeological remains; nearby there are huge saline formations.

82-83 Modern hotels line the shores of the Dead Sea, many of which have thermal baths. The baths offer the benefits of the sea's mineral-rich waters and mud that are used in the production of beauty products. Over recent years, Israel has become a destination for patients from all over the world suffering from chronic sicknesses like rheumatism, psoriasis and asthma.

83 top left At En Boqeq on the Dead Sea south of Masada, numerous modern hotels have been built equipped for thermal cures. Nearly all have thermal baths inside in which the patients undergo strict medical controls before any cure. The hotels also have fresh-water swimming pools and beaches with facilities.

83 top right Generally during spring, it is possible to find brilliant flowers and small patches of green along the shores of the Dead Sea and scattered across the mainly barren mountains. Strips of vegetation can survive thanks to small underground springs and wadis which turn into rushing streams when it rains.

The yellow clay and gentle hills on which Jerusalem stands is the signal that this is the start of the large desert of Judaea. This desert seems to reach its tentacles as far as the southern edges of the Holy City. Travelling south past Bethlehem and Hebron, the desert descends 1,250 feet in only twelve miles to reach the level of the Dead Sea. It is a barren area but has had a continuous human presence since ancient times. The proximity to Jerusalem induced Christian hermits to live in the ravines from the 3rd century AD. They spent six days in the caves praying, meditating, weaving baskets, eating herbs and cane pith, then spent the seventh day at a monastery for the night prayers and the Eucharist. Even today many of these monasteries built into the rocks are inhabited. The largest one is the monastery of St. Saba in the Kidron valley, strictly out of bounds to women. The most attractive is the monastery of Quarentena on the Mount of Temptation. In this area there is certainly no lack of archaeological or historical remains: it is enough just to cite Qumran, Herodium, Masada and Sodom. The Judaean desert runs along the west coast of the Dead Sea, the basin that holds several world records: apart from being the world's lowest surface point, it has the water with the highest level of salinity and the highest density. It is filled with potassium carbonate, magnesium and bromine as well as table salt and industrial salt. Its waters and mud have been shown to be valuable in the cure of several skin diseases. Recently the Dead Sea has excessively shrunk in size: its growing rate of evaporation (5 feet per year) combined with a smaller volume of water reaching it from the river Jordan has lowered the water level by roughly thirty-five feet since 1960. The sea is only dead in name. On its shores stand two chemical plants built during the 1920s to extract magnesium, then the collective farms started to use the desert land to cultivate particular crops and, more recently, ultramodern spas and medical facilities have sprung up. At Ein Ghedi, where Saul reconciled with David when he recognized him as his successor, there is still a series of waterfalls that form small lakes one after another. These provide a pleasant way for the visitor to cool down. The area has now been turned into a large nature reserve.

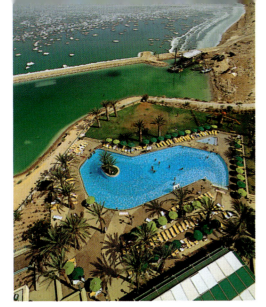

84 top and 84-85 King Solomon's Pillars are found near the ancient mines of Timna north of Eilat on the edges of the Aravà. The unusual rocky formations are 160 feet high; their majestic and surreal appearance is caused by wind erosion and infiltration of water. Not far away, a gigantic sandstone mushroom stands out unexpectedly in the desert.

84 bottom Nature conservation has been one of Israel's main considerations since the state was founded. Strict laws protect nature including even roadside flowers. Many national parks, like Eskol in the photograph, are scattered around the country.

85 top Farming in the desert is the result of a long struggle to exploit the land and water available to best effect. In order to reduce water consumption, advanced techniques to canalize the flow directly toward the plant roots have been introduced, computerized irrigation systems have been designed and cultures of specific species have been increased under cover.

86-87 From Mizpe Ramon, the eye can wander across the huge Desert of Zin at the foot of the immense crater. It is not uncommon to find arches, columns, mushroom shapes and rocks eroded into fantastic shapes by wind and water.

At the southern tip of the Dead Sea where the biblical town of Sodom stood, there is a long strip of savannah called the Aravà. It starts 1,200 feet from the depression and stretches all the way to Eilat, the modern tourist and sea resort on the Red Sea. A good quality road covers this stretch, closed to the east by the brown mountains of Edom in Jordan, and to the west by buttresses close to the Negev desert. Here the area is dotted with kibbutz, which intensively cultivate early produce, and by nature reserves like Hai Bar-Yotvata where all animals present in biblical times have been reintroduced (except for twelve species now extinct).

There is also the Timna nature reserve with the oldest copper mines in the world dating from the 3rd millennium BC and spoken of in the Bible. This is where the amazing columns of King Solomon can be seen, immense purple crests of sandstone 160 feet high created by erosion. Nearby stands the small but attractive Red Canyon.

This strip of the Aravà runs up against the western part of the Negev, the huge desert that covers half of Israel but which is home to only 8 per cent of the population. The city of Beersheba is in the middle. Here past and present live side by side; at the University, technologies for bringing life to the desert are studied - desalination of the water, artificial rain, solar energy - including the extraordinary techniques of irrigation used so long ago by the Nabateans. Not far away the most lovely Bedouin market in Israel is held every week.

From Beersheba the road goes south through another region of kibbutzim. It was to one of these at Sdé Boker that the ex-Prime Minister of Israel, David Ben-Gurion, moved in 1953 to underline the economic potential of this area to the country.

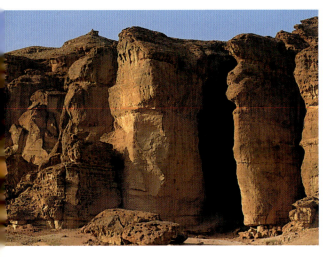

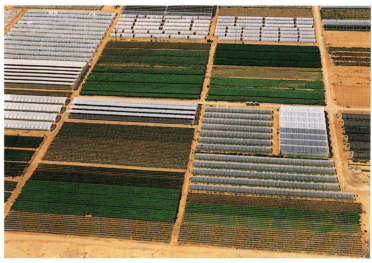

88 top left and 88-89 Mizpe Ramon to the south of Beersheba is the largest of the three craters in the Negev Desert. An astronomic observatory and a visitor center stand on its highest edge, at 3,083 feet, where films and information boards illustrate the extraordinary geological upheavals that have taken place in the area over the centuries.

88 top right and 89 The Negev Desert is rocky to the north but becomes increasingly sandy as it spreads south. It covers 60 per cent of the whole of Israel but offers some of the most attractive landscapes for its variety of geological formations and for the presence of many deep wadis.

89 top Agriculture in the Negev Desert has been a challenge that the Israeli people have fought and won. New methods of irrigation, the search for and the introduction of plants suited to the desert climate have changed the arid land into a garden-like scenery.

89 bottom Two main roads cross the Negev Desert: the first follows the Dead Sea past En Gedi, Masada, En Boqeq and Sodom: it is the faster and more used road; the second one, in the picture, is much more bumpy, it cuts across the desert from Beersheba via Mizpe Ramon and continues south through a landscape of violent colours.

After crossing some sandstone hills and upland plains cut by canals and deep wadis (which are turned into ephemeral but powerful torrents during the winter rains), the countryside changes. Bare, rocky peaks, craters and highlands dotted with rocks stretch as far as the eye can see. This spectacular geological phenomenon measuring twenty-five miles by five is called the Makhtesh Ramon and forms the center of the Negev. In the Jewish language, Makhtesh means 'mortar' but to geologists all over the world it refers to the huge amphitheaters carved out of the youngest rocks by wind and water leaving the older layers open to view in a myriad of colored stripes. If you follow the old Nabatean path down the inside of a crater, you will see limestone layers from 100 million years ago and cross red, yellow and white sandstones to reach, in the center of the amphitheater, formations from 150-180 million years ago. Large black stains of basalt lava from volcanoes active 110 million years ago are to be seen here and there. Also you may come across a hill of perfectly square reddish stone columns like tree trunks cut in a giant saw mill: these are called "the carpenter's shop." They are formed by blocks of quartzite crystallized into prisms by intense heat. In such a setting it seems that life cannot exist, but there are over 1,200 types of plants in this desert and a rich wildlife, some of which has been brought back to the area over the last few decades, such as the Nubian ibex, leopards and wild donkeys.

91 top right Eilat's beach is at the heart of the city in front of the grand hotels and built for the increasing number of tourists. The commercial sea-port is situated at the eastern tip of the shore toward the Jordanian border. It is Israel's only outlet to the southern seas, the Indian Ocean and the Far East.

90 South from Eilat city center there are tourist facilities, hotels and places of unique interest, such as the underwater observatory on the coral beach near Eilat's marine park, and Dolphin Reef.

90-91 and 91 top left Eilat, Israel's most southern city, is known for its warm winters and the richness of the coral reef along the west coast of the Red Sea. The city was founded in 1949 and now attracts tourists from all over the world. All year round they lie on the beaches and stay in its many modern hotels.

In the last part of the desert before reaching the sea, nature changes its appearance once more. Grey and red pointed granite spires are flanked by precipitous ravines in colored sandstone stripes reflected in the sunlight. The glint of the sea appears on the horizon and the visitor arrives at Eilat, the country's most southerly city. Until a few years ago when a modern road was built, this city would appear like a mirage after a long journey down the only path that crossed the desert.

For many Israelis, Eilat is the true "first site" of the Jews as it was here that Moses stopped after the flight from Egypt and where King Solomon settled. The modern city was established in 1949 soon after the birth of the state but without any town planning or particular architecture. The first houses were built on the hills that surround the gulf. The builders had a single aim: to erect as many low-cost flats as possible in the shortest time possible. Different areas sprang up, all inhabited today, which the locals call "Sing Sing" and the "Bastille." From these the city spread during the 1960s toward the hills further inland. These new houses, even if they were more attractive than the original low-cost buildings, were nicknamed *onesh* (punishment) because to reach them on foot from the sea, especially in the summer and with the few means of transport available, was no pleasurable experience.

Over the last twenty years, Eilat has altered its appearance completely. It has now become a main tourist destination for Israelis and foreigners who throng the city all year round. An airport and large modern hotels have been built, the beaches are equipped with sub-aqua facilities along the coral reef that runs the length of the Red Sea and which is the area's real attraction. Along the reef, now an Israeli nature reserve, one of the world's most important underwater observatories has been established. From inside the observatory it is possible to watch one of the last marine environments still uncontaminated by man.

92 top and center At Eilat, even non-divers can admire the beauty and richness of the life of the Red Sea: a yellow submarine takes 47 passengers down to the depth of 197 feet to discover the marvels and extraordinary variety of life in this underwater world.

92 bottom One of the many marine attractions at Eilat is taking a dip at Dolphin Reef: here you can swim in the company of gentle, playful dolphins.

92-93 and 93 right The wonderful mother-of-pearl and colored fishes of the Red Sea can be admired when diving or through the large windows of the underwater observatory.

93 top left The Red Sea coast starting at Eilat is bordered by the coral reef. This is made by the skeletons of special polyps and it can only be found in unpolluted waters at a temperature above 18°C, with fixed salinity and lots of sunlight. The coral grows quickly and becomes an ideal habitat for many marine species.

94 left Each year thousands of tourists from around the world come to the Red Sea to admire its extraordinary forms of life. More than anyone else, it is the underwater divers who can most appreciate the marvels to be found in these waters. The following can be identified in the photograph, from the top: a clownfish with a sea anemone which protects it from any predator, a grouper in his red livery with blue spots and an elegant pterois, easily recognized by its delicate but spiny feathered fins.

94 top right Thanks to the hot and constant water temperature and the abundance of plankton in the Red Sea, many sea creatures have a successful existence, like these alcyonarians.

94 bottom right Even in shallow waters, the Red Sea amazes with the variety and colors of its residents. The photograph shows a couple of shy butterfly fishes with their unmistakable yellow bodies and dark ring around their eyes.

95 The Red Sea coral reef is the scene of an unending competition for space between sea creatures. The photograph illustrates the different extraordinary forms of life whose existences are continuously intertwined: here we see the minuscule orange anthias, the larger squirrelfish, and the flagfish colored with yellow and black stripes; but brightly colored sponges, fan-tailed gorgonians and arborescent alcyonarians are also part of the color palette of the Red Sea.

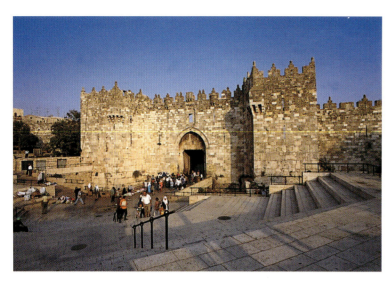

JERUSALEM, CENTER OF THREE WORLD RELIGIONS

96 top left Damascus Gate is the largest, most beautiful and most crowded gate of the Old City. A market is held under it every day. The gate was built as the city's main entrance but without forgetting defensive capabilities, which is why it is flanked by two towers.

96 top right St. Stephen's Gate is on the eastern side of the city. It was built in 1538-39 and set with two lions from the time of the Mameluke sheikh Baibars (1260-77) for which it was called the Lion Gate. According to Christian tradition, Stephen was dragged out of the original gate and martyred.

96-97 Jerusalem is spread over a group of hills about 2,500 feet high which are part of the range that extends across Judaea. The layout of the city streets is very complex and roads and houses have been built to suit the nature of the land.

97 top Jerusalem's walls as they appear today were built by Suleiman the Magnificent between 1536-42. They have been moved and altered over the centuries but their grandeur, battlements, towers and walkways have been maintained.

97 center The Golden Gate in the eastern wall of the Temple area has been walled in, but is visible from the inside. It was built in the 4th century.

97 bottom The valley of Kidron is traditionally a burial place. At the height of the southern city walls stands a line of four remarkable tombs from the 1st century BC. They probably belonged to affluent, maybe priestly, families; Jehoshophat, Assalon, Bnei Hezir and Zaccharia are buried here.

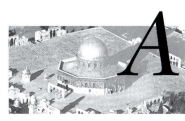

A great historian once wrote that in Jerusalem "faith is inescapable." Visitors to the city finds this out for themselves. They may have a tourist guide with him but before long faith takes the upper hand and guides Their eyes and steps. Almost inevitably it will take them to buildings, houses, roads, courtyards, stones, walls and columns that above all are "holy places." Only then are they considered Jewish, Roman, Byzantine, Arab, Crusader, Mameluke or Turkish constructions or of particular architectural interest. And visitors will breathe in the holiness of the city (no one, not even the most agnostic, can escape it). Only then will they grasp the extent of the city's artistic beauty, but sometimes he may just ignore it. To be able to see all the city's "holy hills," it is necessary to go up to David's Citadel next to the Jaffa Gate. The fortress is misnamed because in fact it was one of Herod's palaces. But with its two names it brings to mind more than one thousand years of history covering both the establishment of the first state of Israel and the establishment of Christianity. It is not simply chance that there is a museum of the history of the city inside the citadel. If you turn your back on modern, noisy Jerusalem, a half turn will take in all of the historical and holy part of the city. To the left, the Church of the Holy Sepulcher, then the Wailing

98 top left The Jewish quarter occupies the south-western corner of the Old City. It was won as a result of the 1967 war and only at that time could Israelis start excavations and restoration.

98 bottom left The Franciscan monastery stands near to where the Tower of Anthony once stood and houses the Church of the Flagellation inside.

A medieval chapel used to stand here which was later turned into a stall and then adapted to be a weaving workshop. In 1836 it was given back to the Franciscans by Ibrahim Pasha to be re-opened for worship.

98 top right Many archaeological excavations have been undertaken at the south-western corner of the Temple area.

The white blocks that form the walls were taken from a portico pulled down by the Romans and were used to construct buildings in the period following the construction of the Aqsa Mosque.

98 bottom right During the Mameluke era, the Moslem quarter of the Old City was filled with religious buildings and hospices for pilgrims.

The fountains placed in front of the mosques, like the Sultan's Fountain, were used for purification purposes.

99 The three bazaars in the Old City have been unchanged for centuries. They are spread along three parallel streets from Crusader times along the main Roman and Byzantine north-south road.

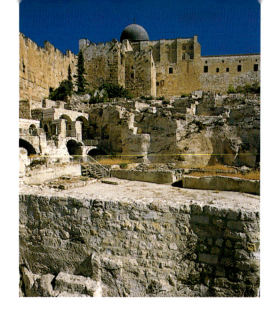

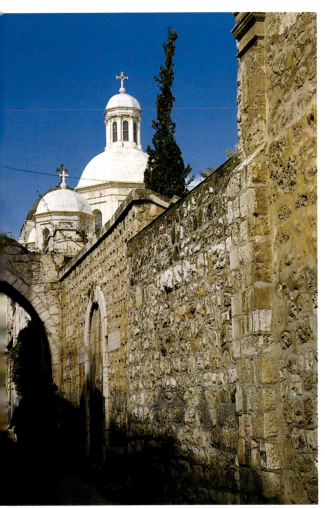

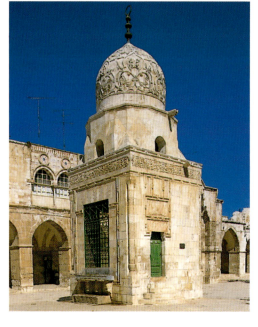

Wall, i.e., what remains of the great temple built by Solomon one thousand years before Christ; next, there is Mount Moriah with the mosques of Omar and Al Aqsa; then, the city of David and Mount Zion with David's tomb and the Last Supper. Further to the right on a long north-south curve, there is the Mount of Olives, the churches of Mary Magdalene and Pater Noster, the Gethsemane, the church of the Assumption, the tombs of the Prophets and the church of St. Peter in Gallicantu.

Historians almost all agree that the name Jerusalem comes from a Semitic root that means to "found," and from the Semitic name for divinity, *shalem*, which contains the concept of peace. The origins of the city are based just outside what is today the southern part of Solomon's wall. It is a triangular area called David's City delimited by Mount Zion, the Gihon Springs and the eastern corner of the Temple plateau. Suleiman the Magnificent left it outside of the present city walls which he had built in the middle 1500's in the white stone of Judaea. The city's origins go right back to the paleolithic era. If they still exist, though, no archaeologist would dare to search for them. Here, every blow of a pick, every stone moved would be considered a profanity against the city's sacred history. All that is known for certain is that already during the 2nd millennium BC there were towers and walls that enclosed and defended a sort of city-state created by a priest-king.

Three constructions naturally attract the observer's attention: the bell tower of the Holy Sepulcher, in the Christian Quarter, and the domes of the two mosques on Mount Moriah. This is the area that the stories and maps drawn by medieval pilgrims called the "center of the world." In a space just a few hundreds of yards square, the three great monotheistic religions have their "holy places," and starting in the 7th century with the Arab conquest, the followers of each religion began to form their own quarters around the holy buildings, just as is true today. The Jews live in the area that faces the Wailing Wall, the Greek and western Christians inhabit the area around the

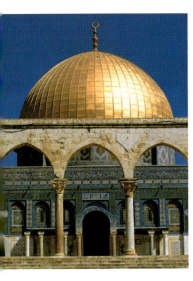

*100 top left
The Dome of the Rock is Islam's holiest site after the Ka'bah in Mecca and the Mosque of the Prophet in Medina. The building stands on a square platform with steps on four sides closed by porticoes where the balances to weigh the souls of the people will be hung on Judgment Day.*

100 center left The octagonal mosque is crowned by a dome plated with pure gold. The lower part of the exterior walls is lined with marble in elaborate patterns while the upper part is decorated with superb majolica tiles from Kashan, with geometric and floral patterns. Tradition has it that it was from this point that Mohammed ascended to heaven.

100 top right The relics of the Prophet are preserved in a square-bottomed tabernacle with gilded grillwork in the Dome of the Rock. The mosque takes its name from the Holy Rock that recalls Abraham's sacrifice and the point in which Mohammed took his flight to heaven leaving his footprint. The structure of the building is unchanged but has been decorated.

100 bottom right The interior of the Dome of the Rock is divided into three concentric ambulatories separated by two rows of columns. The outer one, seen in the picture, is separated from the inner one by 8 pillars and 16 columns. The floors are covered with carpets. The arches are decorated with glass tesserae that come from the original 7th-century structure.

100-101 The columns and pillars inside the Dome of the Rock are placed so as to permit the visitor a clear view of the whole building from any point. The dome is formed by two coves, each supported on 32 ribs which meet at the top. The interior is decorated with floral arabesques painted on plaster.

Church of the Holy Sepulchre, the Armenian and Georgian Christians towards Mount Zion and the Basilica of St. James, while the Moslems live in the angle between the Gate of Damascus and the eastern side of the walls.

The old city can be roughly divided into four districts: the Armenian, the Moslem, the Christian and the Jewish. Each is inhabited by a different community with its own separate life, customs, culture and religion despite living within a few hundred yards of each other. The Armenian quarter is boxed in the south-west corner of the old city and is the first to be seen if one arrives by road from Jaffa. It is silent and peaceful and has been inhabited uninterruptedly by Armenians since the 5th century.

In contrast there is the bustle and vitality of the Moslem district, the largest of the four. It is the best example in the world of an Arab medieval quarter, being almost one enormous souk, a covered market, and it is always filled with tourists. It is formed by two main streets, the Tariq Bab es-Silslieh and the Tariq el-Wad. It is here that the social and commercial life of the Arabs is lived while their religious life has its center at the Temple of Haram esh-Sheriff, the "great holy courtyard," the third most holy place after Mecca and Medina. Here stand the Cupola of the Rock and the El-Aqsa mosque, the second being the more important

102 top The Western Wall is an open-air synagogue where people can be found in prayer at any time of the day, although the males are divided from the females. The Wall is a truly holy place to the Jews and a place of pilgrimage. Often the faithful will insert a note in the cracks of the wall to ask for mercy or express a vow.

102-103 The City of David today includes the Pool of Siloam and extends along the ridge south of the walls of the Temple Area. The city is spread over a series of hills no more than 2,450 feet high and has a complex architectural layout that, expanding from the Old City, has adjusted itself to the contours of the land.

103 top The Western Wall, or Wailing Wall, is a section of the wall that enclosed Solomon's Temple, destroyed by the Romans, in AD 70. The Wall has a great symbolic value because, being the last part of the wall of the Temple still intact, it represents for modern Jews a strong link with the past.

103 bottom Many Jewish boys, whether Israeli or from abroad, celebrate their Bar Mitzvah in front of the Wailing Wall. This is the ceremony when the thirteen-year-old boy comes of age according to Jewish law. From this moment on he is personally responsible before God for observance of religious precepts and he is able to enter the adult world.

of the two from a religious point of view. Not far away the Museum of Islamic Art is housed in two buildings, one Mameluke and one Crusader, and is the oldest museum in Jerusalem.

The Christian district centers around the Church of the Holy Sepulcher which unites in a single architectural core the site of Christ's death, his burial and resurrection and is therefore the holiest place in the eyes of the Christians. It is the arrival point of the Via Dolorosa with the Stations of the Cross where Christian pilgrims from all over the world relive Christ's Passion with processions and prayers, particularly during the Easter period.

The Jewish area is situated in the south-eastern corner of the old city. It has been completely rebuilt in the white stone of Judaea and is mostly inhabited by the religious Jews who want to be as near as possible to their holiest place: the western wall or the Wailing Wall, the last part of the city walls against which Solomon's Temple stood. For years the Wailing Wall was invoked in prayers but it was only in 1967 that Jews could approach it. Today it has the sacredness of a temple and Jews come to it day and night to pray, leave messages to obtain grace, celebrate bar mitzvahs (the rite that celebrates a boy's entry into adulthood) and the most important Jewish holidays – Rosh Ha-shanah, Yom Kippur, Pesach, Shavout, Sukkot and Hanukkah.

104 top left The Church of All Nations has a large mosaic on its façade showing Jesus in agony in front of God.

104 top center left An olive grove stands alongside the Church of All Nations (or Church of Christ's Agony) built by the Franciscans in 1924 on Gethsemane.

104 bottom center left The Church of the Holy Sepulcher is crowned by a large grey dome erected over the tomb of Christ and by another smaller dome over the Catholicon or Chapel of the Greeks. The original building dates from the Constantinian era but has undergone transformations and rearrangements, particularly during the Crusades.

104 bottom left and bottom right The Holy Sepulcher is the Christians' holiest site joining the places of Jesus' death, burial and resurrection in one building.

104 top right Each Christian creed has its own section inside the Holy Sepulchre and the opportunity to celebrate its own rites individually.

105 The property of the Church of the Holy Sepulcher is divided between the different Christian creeds. Rights to the various parts of the church, the internal chapels and even furnishings were the subject of dispute for centuries; only in recent times has an agreement been reached on equal division between the different creeds.

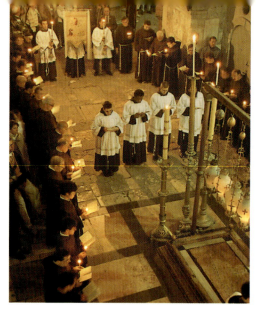

Here history and religion throughout the centuries even seem to have impregnated the stones themselves: in the name of the one and only God, wars have been fought, treaties signed, brutally violent massacres carried out and acts of great generosity performed in this network of lanes and alleys. In 638, the caliph Umar ibn al-Knatthab visited the Church of the Holy Sepulcher dressed as a humble nomad and covered by a patched cloak. He prayed, but outside the building so that his followers would not transform it into a mosque. Then he went up onto Mount Moriah and, upset by the dreadful state of the place where Solomon's temple had once stood, he and his followers removed the layer of rubbish which covered it. Less than fifty years later, a mosque stood there, today is called Omar's mosque. On July 15th 1099, the Crusaders overran the walls of the city and advanced massacring almost all the Moslem and Jewish inhabitants. They reached Mount Moriah where they carried out the most horrific slaughter and then went on to the Church of the Holy Sepulcher.

Today, under the covered market, whose crossed vaults are still the mark of Crusader architecture, the shops sell plastic toys and jeans but nothing has really changed. At dusk on Friday the noises quieten, the streets are less busy and everyone turns to God with the words, sounds and ways handed down from their forefathers. The Jews turn to the Wailing Wall, the Moslems head to the call of the muezzin and the Christians are drawn to the sound of the bells.

Given the enormity of what is represented by and what happens inside Suleiman's walls, the other Jerusalem seems strange and faraway. A single element links the two - the white stone of Judaea that covers every building and which slowly takes on a golden patina to end up as the color of the city. But this is a huge, diverse place, sometimes impersonal, with districts scattered over ten or so small hills. Toward the west the mildness of the Mediterranean climate and nature is hinted at while toward the east the inclemency of the desert of

106 top left The Abbey of the Dormition was consecrated in 1910 and entrusted to the German Benedictine monks of the Congregation of Beuron in Germany, but since 1957 a smaller basilica has been built and the monks are under the authority of Rome. The church commemorates the spot where, according to tradition, Mary died. In the crypt there is a sculpture of Mary on her deathbed.

106 bottom left Inside the Church of the Assumption of the Madonna lies the tomb of the Virgin. This had been a Franciscan church since 1363 but was taken from them in 1757 and is now the common property of the Greek Orthodox and Armenian churches. The tradition linked to the site is that Mary's body was placed above the rock which eroded over the centuries to form the place of devotion today.

*106 right
In Jerusalem, the Orthodox Christians administer a large part of the Holy Sepulcher and half of Calvary while in Bethlehem they tend the Church of the Assumption.*

Judaea is suggested in the mesh of streets that choke the hills in a cobweb of spirals.

The heart of modern Jerusalem is in the pedestrian zone which stretches for several hundred yards from Ben Yehuda to Zion Square and its side streets. This is where the young come to meet and browse in the shops selling clothes, shoes, gifts, books, newspapers etc. It is a good place to shop or to sit in the open air cafés while listening to the radio or making calls on the mobile phone, now almost a physical attachment to all Israelis.

If the old city is the capital of three religions, the modern city is uniquely the capital of the modern state of Israel. As if to emphasize the fact, the State has wrapped the city in forests and encircled it with its most prestigious institutions. The Hebrew University on Mount Scopus to the north, just past the Mount of Olives, dominates the old city from on high. It was from this point that whoever wanted to conquer the old city from the times of Nebuchadnezzar on would start the final assault. To the west stand the Museum of Jewish Art and the Zoological Gardens. The Zoo is truly curious but the visitor who understands the significance of the city will comprehend it without difficulty: it is the biblical Zoo which accommodates birds, mammals, reptiles and insects that are mentioned in the Old Testament. Heading south we find the most representative buildings of the State. The first is the Palace of the Nations, the seat of large cultural and political manifestations in the city. It stands exactly where the Tenth Roman legion was quartered and where later a church and a Byzantine monastery were built. Further south stands the Knesset, the Israeli parliament inaugurated in 1966. It is decorated with cut-glass windows by Marc Chagall and contains the declaration of independence. Next door, beside each other, come the other great university and the Museum of Israel, which contains in fact three separate museums: the Shrine of the Book, with the Dead Sea scrolls, the Archaeological and Biblical Museum,

107 During the 14th century, the keys to the Holy Sepulcher were held by a Moslem who had to allow equal access to Christians of different creeds, each of which claimed equal rights and often caused brawling to take place.

107 top right The church of St. Mary Magdalene near Jerusalem falls under the jurisdiction of the "Church of Russian

Emigration" whose spiritual center is the Metropolita, based in Jordanville, USA.

107 bottom right David's Tomb is situated on the lower floor of the Chapel of the Last Supper. The tomb contains a cenotaph from Crusader times which is much venerated by the Jews. Excavations in 1951 showed that the Tomb stands over another building, maybe a synagogue-church, belonging to a Judaeo-Christian community. Infact, the building has a niche for the Ark of the Covenant facing east.

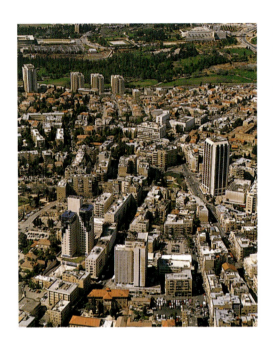

and the Fine Arts Museum. Toward the west, in the heart of the forest of Jerusalem, the State has raised the two buildings of major importance destined to keep historical memories alive: the tomb of Theodore Herzl, founder of Zionism, and the Yad Veshem. Herzl's tomb is situated in the highest point of the city; on the north side of Mount Herzl stands the Military Cemetery containing the graves of the six thousand Israelis killed in battle.

Yad Veshem is a monument to the memory of the six million Jews who were the victims of Nazism. Here are stored documents, photographs, accounts and archives of Hitler's persecution and of the Jewish communities destroyed under Nazism. When the visitor leaves the museum, he finds himself passing along the Avenue of the Righteous in which each tree that lines it records the name of someone who risked his life to protect and save Jews during the years of persecution.

108 top left Next to the walled Old City there is a modern section of Jerusalem similar to a European city. Here the residential buildings are often skyscrapers and the straight, anonymous streets are filled with chaotic traffic.

108 bottom left Ben Yehuda Street is the commercial center and meeting point of the new part of Jerusalem. The street is now a pedestrian precinct filled with shops of all kinds, local craftshops for antique and modern articles, street cafës, restaurants and clubs. This area is crowded day and night with locals and tourists.

108 top right and 109 The building housing the Shrine of the Book is part of the Israel Museum. Its roof is in the form of a jar-lid. The building contains the manuscripts found in 1947 in the caves at Qumran near the Dead Sea, the Dead Sea Scrolls, and the fifteen letters found at En Gedi on the west bank of the Dead Sea in 1960.

108 center right Mount Herzl is Jerusalem's highest point. It is dedicated to Theodor Herzl, founder of Zionism. On the top of the mountain is his black marble tomb and at the entrance to the park stands the Herzl Museum. The military cemetery on the northern side of the mountain honors the 6,000 Israelis who have died in battle.

108 bottom right Yad Veshem, "a monument and a name," stands on the Hill of Remembrance (Har Hazikaron) not far from Mount Herzl. It is dedicated to the six million Jews who lost their lives in the Holocaust. An eternal flame burns in the Hall of Remembrance. On the marble floor the names of twenty-two of the most important death camps are engraved.

CITIES FROM THE BIBLE AND CITIES OF THE FUTURE

110 top left Arad was created in the eastern Negev only in 1961 for the extraction and distribution of phosphates and gas. Today it has 12,000 inhabitants and a university; it is also an important medical center for the cure of asthma due to its dry climate. The area was inhabited in ancient times as is shown by the remains at Tel Arad.

110 bottom left Eilat is the southernmost city in Israel and is the country's only port on the Red Sea. It was founded in 1949 and soon became a major commercial center. It has been a free port since 1985. It can boast no remains of the past but today it is an international tourist resort thanks to its pleasant climate, warm sea and almost intact coral reef.

Israelis love to live in cities. More than 90 per cent of them live in urban areas. Many cities are built in areas inhabited since ancient times like Safed, Beersheba, Tiberias and Akko. Others, like Rehovot, Hadera, Petah Tikva and Rishon Le-Zion were farming villages at the beginning of the 19th century but have now been developed into sizeable towns. And others, like Carmiel and Kiriat Gat, were originally built during the 1950s to house new immigrants but were positioned away from the established routes to spread the population more evenly around the country.

Thanks to the efficient road transportation system, the traveler has no difficulty in moving from one city to another and is able to take in the large differences between the individual centers. For example, ancient Akko still has a natural port surrounded by walls built by the Turks. There is also the white mosque, the caravanserai and the complex which belonged to the Order of the Knights of St. John. Moving to Galilee, the traveler arrives at Tiberias on the lake from where the river Jordan springs. The city has ancient remains that are now protected in an archaeological park. It contains the remains of the biblical Hammat Teverya and, in the area of the synagogue, the beautiful mosaic showing the signs of the zodiac, labeled with their Jewish names. Tiberias is known by Christians because much of Jesus' public life was spent on

110 right Beersheba stands on a wide, almost barren plateau on the edge of the Negev. Up until the beginning of the century it was a small center frequented by Bedouins who lived in the northern Negev. Since the founding of the state of Israel in 1948, the city has grown enormously and has become the most important commercial, industrial and university city in the region.

111 top Netanya, the modern capital of the district of Sharon, was founded in 1929. It was designed with wide avenues and beautiful parks for which it is considered a garden city.

It is called the Pearl of Sharon and today is a bathing resort. Since the end of the 1930s it has become an important center for diamond cutting and polishing.

111 bottom Herzliya was named after Theodor Herzl, the founder of Zionism. It was founded in 1924 by a small group of American Jews who created a moshav,

a collective farming co-operative, along the coast. The city then turned into an industrial center and is now a bathing resort frequented especially by Israeli writers and actors.

its shores but of course it is not the only place: there is also Nazareth, with its Basilica of the Annunciation, the Franciscan monastery and the Fountain of the Virgin which together with Bethlehem and Jerusalem makes up the three holiest Christian cities.

At the start of the Negev Desert stands the city of Beersheba which combines the most ancient history (Abraham's Well is supposedly here) with the futuristic present (the university has advanced research centers). After Beersheba the desert seems to stretch on forever so that when the traveler arrives at the Red Sea, Eilat appears as if in a mirage: modern hotels overlook the beach and coral reef. On this part of the coastline, now a natural park, the visitor can see sharks, dolphins, giant tortoises and turtles in enormous pools. Entering the large underwater observatory below the surface in the marine museum, the visitor can see the multi-colored fish that live on the reef and the hundreds of fish, sponges, coral and other species that live in the Gulf of Eilat.

Today Israel has only two cities with over half a million inhabitants, Jerusalem and Tel Aviv, followed by eleven with more than 100,000 residents (Haifa is the most heavily populated with 270,000). Another fifteen have fewer than 100,000. Israel is home to a number of cities that are unique in the world. They are both very ancient and very modern at the same time; old centers with a souk and narrow streets exist side by side with the modern districts of the city, with the two sometimes separated by no more than a large road. The newer section will have blocks of flats, large shopping centers, sporting facilities and gardens. Many of these cities are to be found in the Negev Desert and were designed to take advantage of the desert's resources. Arriving at these cities after a long trip across the desert is like seeing a mirage. This is how Arad is first perceived, the central city of a group of new towns near the Dead Sea. These towns and others like Beersheba, Yeroham and Dimona (where Israel's first nuclear reactor was constructed) were built from nothing in the 1960s.

Ancient Arad dates back 5,000 years while modern Arad is an example of a new fortress city designed to weaken the strength of the desert wind and heat. All buildings center on squares, the streets are shaded by buildings, and parks and gardens are located in one area to limit water consumption; but the town planning was not completed when the city was built and today there is a uniform network of roads that all meet at a large shopping center.

Thanks to the dry air of the desert, Arad is considered an ideal place to cure asthma, so that it is dotted with hotels and specialist medical facilities. King Uzziah said in the Bible: "Build towers in the wilderness." Arad has been built just a short distance from where Uzziah built his own city and now the blocks of flats of the modern city are the new "towers in the wilderness." The two Arads are the symbol of modern-day Israel: a modern society reborn where the ancient one used to exist.

HAIFA, THE CITY THAT WORKS

112 top left Haifa's coastline has a sandy beach and is much frequented by tourists for its beauty, luminosity, sheltered position and mild climate. Mount Carmel rises behind the beach.

112 bottom left Haifa is made up of three separate areas: the lower city around the port which is the old part of Haifa, the intermediate level around the Technion which is now a lively commercial area, and the upper city on Mount Carmel which is mainly residential with villas and gardens.

112 right Haifa is an important university center famous for its Technion (polytechnic) founded by German immigrants in 1912 as a technological institute. A modern Technion, also for scientific subjects, has been built alongside the old building and this has been joined by a new university (1970) for humanities studies and by a marine studies center.

113 left The port of Haifa was created during the period of the British Mandate. Today it is the second busiest seaport after Ashdod.

An Israeli saying is that "Tel Aviv plays, Jerusalem prays and Haifa works." Haifa is called the "red city" because it has long been considered the strong point of the trades' union movement and, thanks to its ancient port, the country's main industrial city. To the north it is surrounded by petrochemical plants, refineries and small factories, many of which produce high technology goods. Haifa boasts the Technion (the polytechnic) and an important university with 35,000 students.

The city is built on the sides of Mount Carmel in three distinct sections: the lower part is based around the port and two large arterial roads, the Yaffo and the Ha'atzma'ut (Independence Road). The northern zone of the lower city was originally the old commercial area which has now been transformed for modern business. It has expanded to envelop the ancient village of Bat Galim, now a bathing resort, and has created a large industrial suburb to the east.

The middle city stands between two and four hundred feet above the sea. It is called Hadara Ha Carmel (or simply Hadara) and has been developed since the opening of the Technion in 1925. It is the commercial, administrative and cultural heart of the city, but it is also a lively area.

The upper city is Carmel at eight hundred feet above sea level. It is a residential area with parks and gardens that make Haifa the greenest city in Israel. It has villas and elegant hotels connected with other parts of the city by narrow, twisting streets from which the view north toward Akko can be admired.

If one goes right to the top of the mountain, it is possible to see as far as the Lebanese border. The city has always been an example of the peaceful co-existence of Arabs, Druse, Jews and unusual religious groups like the Bahá'i (the latter have their world center here).

Their mausoleum with the large golden cupola tries to combine neo-classical and middle eastern features. Since 1953 it has undisputedly dominated the city landscape.

113 top right Since Israel came into being in 1948, Haifa has always been the example to the rest of the country of the successful cohabitation of Jews, Arabs, Druses and groups of other religions such as the Bahá'i. The various religious orders and sects have full freedom of expression in their synagogues, mosques, temples and churches.

113 bottom right The Shrine of the Báb, on Mount Carmel, was completed in 1953 and hold the remains of the Báb (Arabic for Gate), forerunner of Bahá'u'lláh the founder of the Bahá'i Faith.

JAFFA, THE BEAUTIFUL

114 Jaffa means "beautiful"; the city stretches around the ancient marine port in the picture. Entirely reconstructed, it has taken on the role of Tel Aviv's historical center. Many artists live here, and every evening the antique shops, restaurants and night-clubs in its small streets are filled with Israelis and tourists.

115/118 Taking the road from Tel Aviv to Jaffa, it is not easy to tell when you pass from one zone to the next in this enormous conurbation. The continuity of the seafront between Tel Aviv and the small port of Jaffa differs only in the architecture, as shown in the photographs.

Jaffa is as ancient as Tel Aviv is recent. If the story is true, Jaffa is one of the oldest cities in the world because it was founded by Jiafet, son of Noah, who arrived there forty years after the Flood. Jaffa is the Jewish word for "the beautiful" (Jafo). It stands on a panoramic promontory south of Tel Aviv surrounded by Crusader fortifications. Nearby are the remains of Christian churches like the Franciscan church of St. Peter from 1650, plus Armenian convents and nineteenth-century mosques like Jama El-Baher and La Mahmoudia. The houses in Jaffa were all restored in 1963 and the city today is a residential center for artists. Its streets are lined with art galleries and shops and there are tourist attractions, restaurants and night clubs.

119 The El-Jazzar mosque (or White mosque) was built at Akko in 1781 on the orders of Ahmed el-Jazzar. It stands on the site of an ancient Byzantine basilica which was destroyed in the first Arab invasion (636) and replaced by a mosque which in its turn was razed to the ground by the Crusaders in 1104. The Crusaders then built a church dedicated to St. John on the site of the mosque.

TEL AVIV, THE CITY THAT PLAYS

120 top left Tel Aviv's opera house is one of the most renowned in Israel. The country is very active in the classical music field due to the vitality of its original composers and thousands of musicians, but Israel also boasts a unique and dynamic folk music which is the result of the composite nature of its immigrants.

120 bottom left The 3,000 seater Mann Auditorium is the official home of the Israel Philharmonic Orchestra. The excellent acoustics make it one of the best music halls in the world. This orchestra was founded in 1936 by violinist Bronislav Huberman and has been directed by eminent conductors of the world.

Tel Aviv means the "hill of Spring." It is the liveliest and most cosmopolitan city in Israel. It is an industrial, commercial and financial center with 370,000 inhabitants within the true city limits but 2,500,000 if greater Tel Aviv is considered. Greater Tel Aviv is the connurbation that includes the nearby suburbs and cities of Bat Yam, Holon, Ramat Gan and Bnei Brak and which has been a single community since 1950. Only Jaffa is a separate entity. A quarter of the country's entire population lives in greater Tel Aviv.

Tel Aviv city stretches five miles along the coast and spreads a little over two miles inland. It is the first completely modern Jewish city. Until 1909 when the first houses were built on the edges of ancient Jaffa, the entire area simply contained sand dunes. Since then, the city has expanded continuously in a sometimes chaotic manner to accommodate the growing number of inhabitants.

Tel Aviv's city founders imagined it as a garden city with low buildings built on blocks each surrounded by its own green space. It was created therefore without any proper town planning, but the requirement to provide housing for the Jews fleeing from Europe (only 250 in 1909 but 40,000 in 1926, 70,000 in 1939 and 170,000 in 1940) meant that even the good intentions of the planning department were overruled by the needs of the moment. Next to the original garden city blocks, some of which still exist along Ben Yehuda, the road that runs north-south parallel to the sea, many neo-classical buildings in an eclectic style sprang up during the 1920s that remind one of certain districts in cities like Vienna, Odessa or Warsaw from whence the immigrants arrived. These houses stand on colonnades, with entrances decorated with murals of biblical scenes and with rounded balconies in the European style. They gave the city an original and romantic charm.

During the 1930s, the constructions were based on the international style of the Bauhaus and architects like Le Corbusier and Erich Mendelsohn.

120 top right Ha Yarkon street, one of Tel Aviv's major arterial roads, is lined with modern white blocks of flats, some with original architectural designs, like the one in the photograph.

120 center right This environmental sculpture in the southeast of Tel Aviv by Israeli artist Dani Karavan is called "White Square."

120 bottom right This "Reclining Figure" by Henry Moore is a centerpiece of the large square overlooked by Tel Aviv's Art Museum. The museum, the country's most important for modern art, was opened in 1932 in the house of Meir Dizengoff, the city's first mayor. The current building was designed by Dan Eytan and Yizhak Yashar and was opened in 1971.

121 Ramat Gan, the residential and business center of Tel Aviv, was founded in 1921 by Canadian Jews, who called it Ir Ganim. One of the tallest skyscrapers in the Middle East is located here: Moshe Aviv Tower (on the right in the photograph), also known as City Gate.

122 top left Tel Aviv was founded on the dunes north of ancient Jaffa in 1909 and its name means Hill of Spring. Today it is a modern city that stretches along a sandy coast for 5 miles. A Mediterranean metropolis, it boasts sandy beaches and marinas, and has more than one million inhabitants.

122 center left The sea-front at Tel Aviv is lined with restaurants, bars, gardens and entrances to the beach. It is filled with Israelis and tourists at all hours: in the morning for a jog along the beach, during the day, perhaps during the lunch break, for a dip, and in the evening to enjoy the cooling sea breeze.

122 bottom left Carmel is one of the largest and best known markets in Tel Aviv. It is based in Hacarmel Street near Allenby Street in the center. It is a very rich and colorful market which sells fruit, vegetables and herbs from all regions plus clothes, linenware, shoes and food including the classic pita bread.

122 right In the recent past, Tel Aviv has seen the construction of huge shopping centers like the Opera Tower in the photographs, seen from the outside and from inside the fast food hall. These centers imitate American malls with a wide choice of shops and entertainment facilities.

123 Dizengoff Square in the center of Tel Aviv was named after the city's first mayor, Meir Dizengoff, from whose house the announcement of the birth of the state of Israel was given on 14 May 1948. The main roads of the city converge on the square, around which are modern commercial centers and nightclubs.

The architecture became severe and fundamental, giving the city the appearance that inspired the poet Nathan Alterman to call it "the white city" from the color of its building materials. As a reaction to this style these same buildings were painted in bright colors in the years that followed. Today's buildings are still often blocks of flats on colonnades but now with gardens on the roof.

After the proclamation of the State of Israel on 14 May 1948 from the house of Meir Dizengoff, first Mayor of Tel Aviv, the city began its giddy expansion. To the north it crossed the river Yarkon and to the east it approached the Ayalon. In the 1960s the construction of skyscrapers began, which until then had been utterly foreign to the Mediterranean though today they run all along the Israeli coast. They were built during a period of economic boom when the American-style consumer society had a profound influence on the spartan, pioneering customs of the country.

Today Tel Aviv is filled with chaotic traffic which runs over a thick uniform network of roads starting from the sea which meet large arterial roads running north-south. Like other large western cities, the long streets like Ben Yehuda, Dizengoff and Allenby are lined with shopping centers and skyscrapers containing offices, hotels and restaurants but alongside these there manage to exist local markets and bazaars that still exude a middle eastern atmosphere. Emblematic of this avant-garde city is the diamond industry with its own stock exchange: indeed Israel cuts, polishes and sells eighty per cent of the world's diamonds. Tel Aviv is home to Israel's most diverse lifestyles: modern business, beach relaxation, an animated night life and refined cultural activities spawned by the campus university, the many museums, the theaters and concert halls. The city never seems to sleep, not even on a Saturday when the rest of the country is at rest. Its inhabitants move straight from work to sport, from the office to the theater, from the cinema to the concert hall or meeting room, to end the day in one of the many street bars until, at dawn, the frenetic pace starts up again.

A SINGLE PEOPLE OF A THOUSAND FACES

124 top New Israelis have arrived in the country from all over the world as shown by people's very different facial features. The so-called "Law of Return" gives every descendant of Jews forced abroad by the diaspora the right to come to Israel and obtain citizenship upon arrival. After six million Jews were killed by the Nazi death camps in the Shoah, every Jew now lives in the knowledge that he or she has a safe homeland which offers a safe haven.

124 bottom and 125 top left The entire Yemeni community numbers 50,000 people and was brought to Israel by an eventful air-lift during the 1950s. Its members have retained their customs and continue to wear their traditional clothes, especially at weddings. They say they are the descendants of the Jewish Himyarite kingdom that flourished on the southern coast of Saudi Arabia during the Byzantine era.

Who are the Israelis? Visitors to the country will find an exact answer in the Beth Hatefutsoth Museum on the Tel Aviv campus. This is a historical and ethnological museum that tells of the dispersion of the Jews around the world from antiquity to the present time.

There are no documents, art objects or departments but 3-D models, illustrative panels, theme boards, projection rooms and sound documents for which the most modern multimedia systems available have been used. One of these panels explains the family trees of various real people (living or dead) such as engineers, waiters, office workers, etc., who one might meet in the street.

The people making up the family trees are described by name and sometimes photograph and the visitor can see the extraordinary confluence of backgrounds that led to one subject of the family tree. One of their great-great-grandparents may have been Romanian and the other German, one great-grandparent was perhaps born in Russia and the other in America, their son may have married a Lebanese or Greek girl and had a son born in France or England, and so on until Israel was created, since when children born in the country have been given the nickname "sabra" (prickly pear) to distinguish them from those born outside Israel.

This background would have little resonance in any other country of the

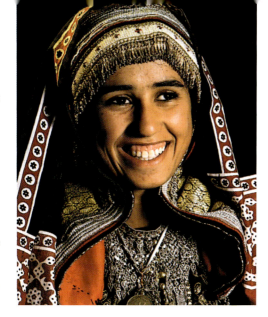

124-125 Many particularly religious Jews live in the Jewish quarter of the old city of Jerusalem, like the family shown in the photograph. This district faces the Western or Wailing Wall and has become the seat of schools of the Talmud that have restarted the ancient tradition of rabbinical studies.

125 top right The Jewish wedding has maintained the same ritual for centuries. In front of two witnesses, the bridegroom slips the ring onto the right forefinger of the bride and declares her his wife. The couple retire under the nuptial canopy where the officiator recites seven blessings in the presence of ten men. The couple drink wine from the same cup which is then broken.

world, where each inhabitant represents a small part of the country's history. But in Israel it is indispensable because here, out of a population of 6.8 millions in a country almost the same size as Wales, less than half of the population can say that their father and grandfather were born there. The rest arrived between 1948 and today from one of the 80 countries that have contributed to immigration: 58 percent from Europe, 18 percent from the Americas and Oceania. There is even one per cent that has no recorded origin! It is not accidental that in the same museum there is a section that reconstructs and documents the family trees of as many Israelis and Jews around the world as possible. Sociologists say that Zionism (the return of Jews to their homeland), the need to survive and to defend constantly the borders of their country have created in a few decades the "new Jew," what they now call the "regular Israeli." The stereotype of the small, dark Jew wrapped in threadbare rags has disappeared: in his place is a tall, smiling, suntanned man or woman with a permanently open collar as happy on a tractor as handling a gun or computer.

Communal life on the kibbutz (collective farm where everything is shared, property and harvest) or in the moshav (co-operative village in which everyone owns their own piece of land but uses a unique sales system of the products and stores)

126 After the foundation of the Jewish state in 1948, many groups of Orthodox Jews started to establish themselves in Jerusalem and began to start schools to study the Talmud. These are now attended even by young children. At the Talmud Torà Shomrei Ha Chomoth in Jerusalem, the youngsters are learning the fundamentals of Hebraism.

126-127 The swearing-in ceremony of the new recruits is one of the most important moments in the life of every young Israeli. Military service is obligatory for men and women above the age of 18. It begins with four months of training, then the men (for three years) and the women (for two) are sent to different units.

127 top left Women are called up to perform military service for twenty months in peace time and are exempted only for religious reasons. They generally carry out logistics and social tasks and are never sent to the front line even in times of war. The army is an important opportunity for Israelis to fraternize, particularly for new immigrants.

127 top right Scientific and technological research is particularly advanced in Israel. Women and men are engaged in research in all types of fields. Many work in institutes that are linked to universities that collaborate on scientific projects with many major nations. The institutes send scholars for work periods abroad, and receive visiting scholars.

have without doubt strengthened the unitary spirit of Jews who have arrived in Israel from all corners of the earth. And perhaps even more strongly felt as the decisive element of cohesion is the obligatory military service for both men and women. Men are called up for three years with annual recalls up till the age of fifty while women serve for two years and can be recalled annually until they are thirty-four.

Probably this is as much of a stereotype as the first example. To start with, the New Jew is all right, but what kind? Ashkenazim or Sephardim? In other words, did this Jew's forefathers from the Middle Ages pray using the central-eastern liturgy (Ashkenaz = Germany) or the one used in the Iberian peninsula (Sepharad = Spain)? This is not just a formal distinction. Ashkenazim also speak a particular language, Yiddish (a German Jewish dialect), that the Sephardim do not know. Sephardim use another language, Ladin (also known as Spagnolito), which is a mixture of Spanish and Hebrew. The different rites do not simply signify different traditions, synagogues and rabbis but also different political leanings with all that follows from that regarding the running of the state and society.

Once this has been established, the image of the New Jew must be considered, for example the Roman craftsman who restores Venetian furniture in the Italian temple in Jerusalem or the ex-Prime Minister who has lost nothing of his Polish accent in sixty years. It would be easier if it were not necessary also to add among the New Jews the nearly 30,000 "falasha," black Ethiopian Jews who immigrated to Israel about ten years ago and who proudly trace their Jewishness back to the meeting of the Queen of Sheba with King Solomon. This is a little exaggerated as historians tell us that their Judaism is really much more recent, dating from the migrations of Jewish tribes from Palestine to the east African coast at the time of the difficulties caused by the Babylonians or at the start of the Christian era. Or then again there are the half million Russians who have arrived since the fall of the Berlin Wall, for many of whom

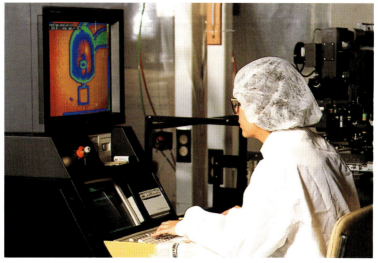

128 top All kinds of strange meetings can take place in front of the Damascus Gate in Jerusalem, like this one with a seller of cold drinks. The Damascus Gate (or Column Gate) faces north; it is one of the eight gates that give entrance and exit to the old city, that is divided into four quarters: Jewish, Christian, Armenian and Moslem.

128 center The Bedouin market in Beersheba every Thursday morning is one of the most colorful and attractive markets in the region. Handmade articles from copper, camel wool and leather can be found here. This market is the only commercial outlet for the desert Bedouins to sell the goods they produce and to buy what they need for their nomadic life.

128 bottom Every Friday morning, along the walls that surround the Old City of Jerusalem, a large Arab animal market is held. Sheep and goats in particular are bought and sold and also the donkeys and camels used by Arab farmers in the fields as beasts of burden and for transport.

128-129 On the expanse of the Dome of the Rock in Jerusalem, also mistakenly called Omar's mosque, thousands of believers gather to pray every Friday. The rock is the highest part of Mount Morian, which is associated with Abraham's sacrifice of Isaac, the apparition of the Angel to David and the night journey of the prophet Mohammed.

129 top left The majority of Arab women continue to wear the traditional long dress and to cover their head with a large scarf. It is common to see Arab women in the streets of Jerusalem in classic Jordanian costumes as they walk beside tourists in modern clothes.

129 top right This Moslem in prayer in front of the Al Aqsa mosque in Jerusalem is performing one of the injunctions, or "pillars," of the Islamic faith. These are the profession of faith, the canonical prayer five times a day, the giving of alms, fasting during the month of Ramadan and the pilgrimage to Mecca at least once in a lifetime.

the Jewish religion was only a faint family memory.

So what is it that has allowed this unusual, if not unique, mixture of radically different physiques, languages, customs, traditions, mentalities and cultures to succeed over the past centuries? The visitor to the museum will recognise it at the end of his visit without need for other explanation: first and most important, religion; second, language, though this for many may simply be a language of prayer; and thirdly, the same exact act of prayer in a synagogue in whatever part of the world they happen to be. And in this century, to these three factors can be added the most cementing of all, Zionism.

The Israelis believe they have created in a few decades what, for example, the United States have not yet achieved in two centuries - a truly multiracial society. It is difficult to say if the objective has really been attained. There is no doubt however that the differences between the Ashkenazin, Sephardim and Jews coming from the Middle East and North Africa often create opposition if not rivalries between them. It must be said however that, unlike other societies where the problem of integrating immigrants exists, the Israelis do not have individuals to deal with who arrive singly looking for a better quality of life, but entire peoples who arrive en masse, on some occasions over a period of just a few days, without physical baggage but loaded with mental and cultural baggage instead - customs, language, traditions etc. One of these groups is the Yemeni whose entire community (about 50,000 people) was airlifted to Israel during the 1950s and in whose traditional history exists the Jewish Himyarite kingdom which flourished on the southern coast of Saudi Arabia in Byzantine times. There are also Moroccan, Tunisian, Libyan, Iraqi, Syrian, Lebanese, Turkish and Iranian Jews who arrived in waves every time Israel was at war with their own Arab countries. It is true that most of them are second generation and are by now almost "regular Israelis" but it is also true that only a quarter of marriages takes place between people of different ethnic backgrounds.

The fact is that in a land like Israel traditions from the past have a large influence on today's life, because there are peoples living there whose names everywhere else only exist in history books, but who are part of everyday life and claim their specific role in society and law. The statistics say that 16 percent of the population are Moslems. Fine, but within that number there are 750,000 Arabs, thirty or so Bedouin tribes (nomads of the Sinai who provided westerners with a name with which to classify all Arabs as the ancient Greeks called them "Sarakenoi" - Saracens) and three thousand Circassians. These too are Moslems but

130 top left There are many pilgrims, particularly Christians, in Israel at all times of the year but especially at Easter and Christmas. They visit the places where Jesus is known to have stopped, one of which is the river Jordan where Jesus was baptized by John.

130 top right Holy Week is a very important time for all Christian pilgrims who come to Jerusalem to walk in procession along the Via Dolorosa. This is the road Jesus followed carrying his cross from the Praetorium to Calvary. The fourteen stations have been marked along the road for the benefit of the Christian faithful; the last five stations are located inside the basilica of the Holy Sepulcher.

130-131 There are roughly 300 members of the Samaritan sect living in Israel. They are divided in two groups, one at Holon and the other one at Shechem near Nablus. Their holy place is Mount Gerizim in Samaria which they say is the true site of the temple. As far as anyone knows, the Israeli Samaritans are the only ones in the world.

131 top An agreement between the various Christian communities for the guardianship of the Holy Sepulcher has existed since 1757. The basilica is divided into three well defined areas which are entrusted to the Franciscans, the Armenians and the Greeks for liturgy and protection. There also exist several other areas for which the Syrian-Jacobites, Abyssinians and Copts have lesser privileges. The photograph shows the guardians of the Holy Sepulcher parading near the Jaffa Gate.

131 center The 72,000 Druse who live in Israel are spread across 22 villages in the north of the country. Their ancestral father, Darazi, wrote the basic texts of their religion in which Gnostic, neo-platonic, messianic and reincarnation principles are merged.

131 bottom Russian Orthodox patriarchs often wear medallions which put one in mind of the sacred icons of their home country.

they keep themselves and their culture very separate from Islamists and Jews with whom they do not want to assimilate at all.

Some of these Moslems (though many are Christian) are the Palestinians who are trying to create, not without difficulty, their own state. Their aim is for a Palestinian state to exist alongside the Jewish one so that what has been called the "Palestinian diaspora" can be put to an end after fifty years.

Although 3 percent of the population (140,000 people) is Christian they are divided into Latins, Greeks, Maronites, Armenians, Syrians, Copts and Chaldeans. Society and law must also account for 15,000 Karaites, a Jewish sect formed in the eighth century in Persia which recognizes the Pentateuch (the first five books of the Bible) as the only valid source of religious law, as a result of which they have their own religious courts and marry exclusively amongst themselves. Furthermore, there are 72,000 Druse, a people which lives in the mountains of the north: they adopted their religion a thousand years ago in Cairo when Darazi, their founder, wrote the basic texts. We know only that their religion is a mixture of gnostic, neo-platonic, messianic and reincarnation influences, but not much more, since a feature of Druse thought is secrecy; only a few of their wise men are party to all the secrets of their religion. They do not permit conversion or marriage outside their community and enjoy complete social, cultural and religious autonomy. They practise the *taqqiya*, a principle of complete loyalty to the government of the country they are living in. At the beginning of the century the city of Haifa was chosen as the center of yet another religious movement that has nothing to do with the area in which it is based: it is the Baha'i faith which was created last century in Persia by Mirza Husain Ali, known as Baha'ullah (Splendour of God) and who, according to himself, is the most recent manifestation of God after Jesus, Mohammed, Zoroaster and Buddha.

Finally, more than four million Israeli Jews have to take into account the three hundred Samaritans who are convinced that they are the only authentic Jews. They say they are descended from the ten tribes of Israel who they believe were never deported to Assyria as stated in the Old Testament. They too recognize the Pentateuch as the only sacred book which they hand down through the generations written in a script that is similar to Phoenician, but they speak Arabic as an everyday language and say that the true temple was not built in Jerusalem on Mount Sion but on Mount Gerizim in Samaria. For all anyone knows, they may be the only Samaritans in the world.

INDEX

Page numbers followed by "c" refer to captions

A

Abd-el-Malik, 34
Abimelech, 59c
Abraham, 21, 21c, 34, 59c, 100c, 111
Abu Bakr, 34c
Abyssinians, 131c
Achziv, 74c
Acre, 40c, 41c, 60, 66c, 68, 110, 112
Aelia Capitolina, see Jerusalem
Ahmed el-Jazzar, 41c, 119c
Akko, see Acre
Al Aqsa, 98c
Alexander the Great, 28, 28c, 31c
Alexandria in Egypt, 29
Allenby, Edmund, 43c
Alterman, Nathan, 122
Ammonites, 24c
Anatolia, 25
Andrew, 62c
Antiochus III Seleucid, 29c
Antiochus IV Epiphanes, 29, 29c
Anthony Tower, 98c
Antiochia, 29c
Arab League, 47
Arabia, 34, 54c
Arad, 110c, 111
Arafat, Yasser, 52, 53c
Aravà, 78, 84, 84c
Archeological and Biblical Museum of Jerusalem, 108
Aristobulus II, 30
Aristotles, 28c
Ark of the Covenant, 24c, 64c, 107c
Armenians, 131c
Asher, tribe of, 25
Ashkelon, 10, 60c, 74
Ashkelon-Zikim, 74c
Assalon, 97c
Assyrians, 54
Asthoreth, 23c
Augustus, 57
Auschwitz, 46c
Avdat, 9, 70, 70c
Ayalon, 122
Ayyubid dynasty, 36c

B

Babylon, 27c, 28
Bahá'i, 112, 113c, 131
Baibars, 68c, 97c
Balfour, Arthur J., 42, 42c, 44c
Banjas, 77c
Banyas, 62, 68c
Bar Am, 10, 10c
Barak, Ehud, 53, 53c
Baram, 62
Bar-Kochkba, 33c
Barlev, 51c
Basel, Congress of, 42c
Basilica of Annunciation (Nazareth), 111
Basilica of St. James, 100
Bat Galim, 112
Bat Yam, 120
Bathsheba, 26c
Be'er-Safad-Be'er Matar, 19c
Beersheba, 19c, 59, 59c, 84, 89c, 110, 110c, 111, 128c
Begin, Menachem, 52, 52c
Belvoir, castle of, 10, 68, 68c, 69c
Ben Gurion, David, 47, 48, 48c, 50, 84
Benjamin, 24c
Benjamin, tribe of, 25
Bet Alpha, 10, 64c
Bet Guvrin, 60c
Bet She'an, 10c, 18, 33c, 62, 62c, 64c, 80
Bet Shearim, 10, 10c, 60c
Bethlehem, 9, 31, 59, 80c, 82, 106c, 111
Bnei Brak, 120
Bnei Hezir, 97c
Bonaparte, Napoleon, 40c, 41, 41c, 60
Book Sanctuary in Jerusalem, 33c, 54, 106, 108c
Buchard, manuscript of, 34c
Buchenwald, 46c

C

Cabal, 80
Caesarea, 10, 10c, 13c, 62, 66c
Calvary, 106c, 131c
Camp David, Treaty of, 52, 52c
Canaan, 18, 21, 22, 24c
Cappadocia, 72c
Carmiel, 110
Carter, James, 52c
Kidron, valley of, 82, 97c
Cerberus, 60
Chagall, Marc, 106
Chapel of St. Nicholas, 72c
Chapel of St. Stephen Protomartyr, 72c
Church of All Nations or of Agony, 104c
Church of the Catholicon, 104c
Church of the Flagellation, 98c
Church of the Holy Sepulchre, 34, 34c, 97, 98, 104c, 131c
Church of the Pater Noster, 98
Church of St. George, 70c
Church of St. Mary Magdalene, 98, 107c
Church of St. Peter (Jaffa), 119
Church of St. Peter in Gallicantu, 98
Church of the Assumption, 98, 106c
Church of The Miracle of the Loaves and the Fishes, 78c
Cisjordan, 52
City of David, 2c, 60, 97, 98, 103c
City of Jerusalem, 2c
Cleopatra, 54, 57
Clinton, Bill, 53c
Constantine, 34
Copts, 131c
Couche, Louis-François, 41c
Cyprus, 25, 46c
Cyrus the Great, 28, 28c

D

Daher el-Omar, 66c, 68c
Damascus, 30
Damascus Gate, 97c, 100, 128c
Dan, 59, 77c
Dan, tribe of, 25
Darazi, 131, 131c
David, 10c, 24c, 25, 26c, 82, 128c
Dayan, Moshe, 50, 51c
Dead Sea, 9c, 10, 13c, 32, 33c, 54, 54c, 57, 57c, 59c, 74, 77c, 78, 82, 82c, 84, 89c, 108, 111
Dead Sea Scrolls, 106, 108c
Deborah, 24c
Dimona, 111

132

Divided Monarchy, 60c
Dizengoff, Meir, 122, 122c
Dolphin Reef, 90c, 92c
Dome of the Rock, 100c
Domenichino (Domenico Zampieri), 21c
Dor, 60, 60c
Dormition, Abbey of the, 106c
Dreyfus, 42, 42c

E

Edom, 84
Edrisi, 39c
Egypt, 21c, 22, 22c, 23c, 26, 29, 36c, 38c, 40c, 41c, 48, 50, 51c, 52, 57, 74, 90
Eilat, 50, 70, 78, 84, 84c, 90, 90c, 92, 92c, 111, 111c
Ein Boqeq, 82c, 89c
Ein Ghedi, 10, 59c, 82, 82c, 89c, 108c
Eytan, Dan, 120C
el-Jazzar, 66c
el-Wad, 18c
el-Walid, 54c
En David, 82c
Ephraim, tribe of, 25
Eskol, 84c
Essenes, 33c
Euphranor, 28c
Euphrates, 18

F

Fine Arts Museum of Jerusalem, 108
Flavian dynasty, 33c
Flavius Silva, 57
Fountain of the Virgin (Nazareth), 111
Franciscan Monastery (Nazareth), 111
Frederick Barbarossa, 36c

G

Gad, tribe of, 25
Galilee, 10, 10c, 37, 50, 59, 60c, 60c, 62, 62c, 64c, 68, 68c, 70, 77, 80, 80c, 110
Gamla, 62

Gaza Strip, see Gaza
Gaza, 9, 37, 51c, 52, 53c, 74, 131
Gethsemane, 98, 107c
Gezer, 18, 70
Ghedalià, 26
Gihon, 98
Gilboa, 24c
Gilead, 78
Ginnosar kibbutz, 78c
Golan, 10, 50, 51c, 62c, 68c, 77, 77c
Golden Gate, 97c
Golgotha, 34c
Greeks, 131c
Gros, Antoine-Jean, 41c

H

Ha Lashon, 9c
Hadera, 110
Hadrian, 32, 33c
Haganah, 45
Hai Bar-Yotvata, 84
Haifa, 44c, 47c, 48, 48c, 60, 60c, 74c, 111, 112-113, 131
Hammat, 10c
Hammat Gader, 10, 62c
Hammat Teverya, 110
Hammat Tiberias, 64c
Hanukkah, 103
Har Hazikaron, 108c
Haram esh-Sheriff, 100
Hashani, 77c
Hatefutsoth, Beth, 124
Hathor, 23c
Hazor, 18, 19c, 60c, 70
Hebron, 82
Heraclius, 34, 66c
Hermon, 77, 77c
Herod Antipas, 31c
Herod the Great, 10c, 13c, 30, 34c, 54, 57, 57c, 59, 60c, 66c, 97
Herodion, 10, 72c
Herodium, 59, 59c, 82
Herzl Museum, 108c
Herzl, Theodor, 42, 42c, 108, 108c, 111c
Herzliya, 111c
Hishsam, 10
Hitler, Adolf, 44
Holon, 19c, 120, 131c

Holy City, see Jerusalem
Holy Land, 2c, 36c, 40c
Holy Rock, 100c
Holy Sepulcher, 100, 103, 104, 106c, 107c, 131c
Horns of Hattin, 69c
Huberman, Bronislav, 120c
Hula, valley of, 77, 77c, 78
Hussein of Jordan, 53c
Hussein Selim El-Hussein, 43c

I

ibn Abd al-Malik, 10
Ibraim Pascià, 98c
Indian Ocean, 90c
Iraq, 18, 48
Isaac, 21, 21c, 34
Isaiah, 54
Isham, 35c, 54c
Israelites, 24c
Issachar, tribe of, 25

J

Jacob, 21, 21c, 22
Jaffa, 19c, 34c, 41c, 114-119, 120, 122c
Jaffa Gate, 2c, 97, 100, 131c
Jaffet, 119
Jehoshophat, 97c
Jeremiah, 27c
Jericho, 9, 10, 18, 35c, 54, 54c, 72c
Jeroboam, 26
Jerusalem, 2c, 9, 13c, 18, 24c, 26, 26c, 27c, 28, 29, 29c, 30c, 31c, 32, 33, 34, 34c, 36c, 37, 37c, 40c, 41, 43c, 44c, 47, 47c, 48, 49c, 51c, 57, 60, 60c, 62, 68, 72c, 80c, 82, 97-108, 111, 112, 125c, 126, 126c, 128c, 131, 136c
Jewish Art Museum of Jerusalem, 106
Jewish Colonial Bank, 43c
Jezreel, valley of, 80, 80c
John, 131c
John Hyrcanus, 30
John of Damascus, 72c
Jordan, 48, 52, 53c, 68, 70, 78, 84, 90c

Jordan river, 9, 9c, 10, 47, 62, 68, 68c, 74, 74c, 77, 77c, 78, 82, 110, 131c
Joseph, 22, 22c
Joseph, Jacques François, 41c
Josephus, 57
Joshua, 24c, 25, 54
Judaea, 19c, 26, 31c, 32, 33c, 54, 54c, 59c, 72c, 78, 80, 82, 97c, 98, 103, 104, 106
Judaea, tribe of, 25

K

Kapharnoum, 10, 62, 62c, 78c
Karavan, Dani, 120c
Kashian, 100c
Khirbet el-Mafiar, 35c
Kidron, 72c
Kinneret, see Lake of Tiberias
Kiriat Gat, 110
Kléber, 40c
Knights of the Teutonic Order, 68c
Korazim, 62
Koziba, 72c
Kurzi, 62

L

Lake of Tiberias, 62c, 74c, 77c, 78, 78c, 80c
Latrun, 60c
Le Corbusier, 120
Lebanon, 26, 39c, 74
Likud, 52
Lion Gate, 97c
Lucilius Bassus, 59

M

Majdal Shams, 77c
Makhtesh, Ramon, 89
Mamshit, 9, 70, 70c
Manasses, tribe of, 25
Masada, 10, 13c, 32, 54, 57, 57c, 59, 77c, 82, 82c, 89c
Mausoleum of the Báb, 113c
Mediterranean Sea, 9, 18, 29, 30, 41, 54, 60, 70, 80c, 106

Megiddo, 18, 60, 60c, 80
Meir, Golda, 48c, 50
Mendelsohn, Erich, 120
Merneptah, 22
Mesopotamia, 18
Mirza Husain Ali, 113c, 131
Mishnà, 32
Mizpah, 24c
Mizpe, Ramon, 84c, 89c
Moab, 78
Mohammed, 34, 34c, 54c, 100c, 128c
Monastery of Mar Saba, 72c
Monastery of Quarentena, 72c, 82
Monastery of St. Catherine, 34c
Monastery of St. George of Koziba, 72c
Monastery of St. Saba, 72c, 82
Monfort, castle of, 10, 68c
Moore, Henry, 120c
Moses, 22, 72c 90
Mosque of El-Jazzar (Acre), 119c
Mosque of Jama El-Baher (Jaffa), 119
Mosque Mahmoudia (Jaffa), 119
Mosque of Al Aqsa, 98, 103, 128c
Mosque of Omar, 98, 104
Mount Carmel, 40c, 60, 66c, 74c, 112, 112c, 113c
Mount Gerizim, 131, 131c
Mount Herzl, 108, 108c
Mount Meron, 80
Mount Moriah, 98, 104, 128c
Mount of Olives, 34c, 106
Mount of the Beatitudes, 78c
Mount of the Temptation, 82
Mount Scopus, 106
Mount Tabor, 41c, 80, 80c
Mount Zion, 34c, 98, 100, 131
Museum of Islamic Art of Jerusalem, 103

N

Nabateans, 70, 70c
Nablus, 131c
Nahal Keziv, 68c
Nahal Mishmar, 19c
Nahalal, 80c
Nahariya, 47c, 74c
Naphtali, tribe of, 25
National Jewish Fund, 43c
National Museum of Israel of Jerusalem, 18c, 19c, 23c, 54, 106, 108c
Nazareth, 9, 10, 60, 80, 80c, 110
Nebi Musa, 72c
Nebuchadnezzar II, 26, 27c, 106
Negev, 9, 9c, 19c, 54, 59, 59c, 70, 70c, 84, 89, 89c, 110c, 111, 126c
Nelson, Horatio, 40c, 41c
Netanya, 74, 110c
Netanyahu, Benjamin, 53
Nile, 22, 41c
Nimrud, 10, 68c
Nineveh, 68c
Noah, 21c , 119
Nubia, 89

O

Oboda, 70c
Old City 98c, 103c, 108c
Omayyad dynasty, 35c, 54c
Order of Hospitallers, 69c
Order of St. John, 66c, 110
Order of Templars, 68c

P

Palace of Isham, 54c
Palestine, 10c, 25, 28, 29, 30, 32, 32, 34, 37, 39c, 41, 42, 42c, 43c, 45, 45c, 46c, 47, 126
Parthians, 57
Peres, Shimon, 52, 53c
Persia, 28
Persian Gulf, 41
Pesach, 23c, 104
Petah Tikva, 110
Peter, 62c, 78c
Peter the Hermit, 36c
Petra, 9, 70
Philip II of France, 36c
Philip of Macedonia, 28c
Philistines, 24c
Phoenicia, 29c
PLO, 53c
Pompey, 30
Pontius Pilate, 33c, 34c
Poussin, Nicolas, 24c
Ptolemy, 29
Hadrian, 32, 33c

Q

Qazrin, 62c
Qish, 18
Queen of Sheba, 26c, 126
Qumran, 10, 33c, 54, 54c, 82, 108c

R

Rabin, Yitzhak, 52, 53, 53c
Ramallah, 52c
Ramat Gan, 120
Ramesses II, 22, 60c
Ramla, 70
Red Canyon, 84
Red Sea, 9, 23c, 34, 70, 78, 84, 90c, 92, 92c, 94c, 111, 111c
Rehoboam, 25
Rehovot, 110
Richard the Lionheart, 36c
Rishon Le-Zion, see Petah Tikva
Roberts, David, 2c
Romans, 29c
Rome, 30, 30c, 31, 31c, 33c, 54, 57, 62
Room of the Last Supper, 34c, 98, 107c
Rosh Haniqra, 74c
Rosh Hashanah, 104
Ruben, tribe of, 25

S

St. Jean d'Acre, 36c
St. Saba, 72c
St. Stephen's Gate, 97c
Sadat, 52, 52c
Safed, 37, 80, 110
Saladin, 10, 36c, 68, 69c
Samaria, 68, 78, 80, 131, 131c
Samuel, 24c, 25
Sanctuary of Beatitudes, 9c
Sanzio, Raffaello, 21c, 22c, 23c
Sargon II, 26
Saul, 24c, 25, 82
Schnorr, Julius von Carolsfeld, 23c
Scythopolis, 10c, 33d
Sdé Boker, 84
Sea of Galilee, see Lake of Tiberias
Seleucids, 29
Seleucus III, 29c
Sepphoris, 62, 64c
Sessbasar, 28c
Seti I, 22
Shalem, 98
Sharon, 51c, 53, 110c
Shavout, 104
Shechem, 131c
Shivta, 9, 70, 70c
Shoà, 124c
Shrine of the Book, 106
Sichem, 18
Siloam, 60
Simeon, tribe of, 25
Sinai, 18, 22, 50, 51c, 52, 70c, 128
Sobata, 70c
Sodom, 82, 84, 89c
Solomon, 25, 26, 26c, 70, 84, 90, 98, 126
Solomon's Pillars, 84c
Solomon's Temple, 29, 32, 34, 34c, 103, 104
Star of Jordan, see Belvoir castle
Stephen the Thaumaturge, 72c
Stephen, 97c
Suez Canal, 50, 51c
Sukkot, 104
Suleiman the Magnificent, 97c, 98, 104
Syria, 10, 18, 28, 29, 29c, 32, 36c, 48, 51c, 131
Syrian-Jacobites, 131c

T

Tabgha, 78c
Talmud, 32
Tariq Bab es-Silsileh, 100
Tariq el-Wad, 100
Tel Arad, 110c
Tel Aviv, 51c, 53, 60c, 74, 74c, 111, 112, 114c, 119, **120-122**, 124
Tel Aviv Art Museum, 120c
Tell el-Ajjul, 23c
Tell es-Sultan, 54c
Temple of Jerusalem, 24c, 26c, 28c, 29c, 33c, 51c, 60c, 97c, 98, 98c, 100, 103c
Theotokos, 72c
Tiberias, 9, 10, 10c, 31c, 64c, 78, 110
Tigris, 18
Timna, 70, 84, 84c
Tiran, 34, 50, 51c
Titus, 30c, 31c, 32, 33c, 57
Tomb of David, 107c
Tomb of St. Saba, 72c
Torah, 26c
Tower of Stratone, 13c
Tyre, 26

U

Umar ibn al-Khatthab, 104
Uzziah, 111

V

Vespasian, 33c
Via Maris, 10, 60c, 78c

W

Wailing Wall, 97, 98, 102c, 103, 103c, 104, 125c
Washington, Treaty of, 52, 52c
Weizmann, Chaim, 48, 48c
West Bank, 51c, 52, 131

Y

Yad Vashem, 108, 108c
Yadin, Yigael, 60c
Yarkon, 122
Yarmuk, 62c
Yashar, Yizhak, 120c
Yechiam, 10c
Yehi'am, 68c
Yeroham, 111
Yigal Allon, 78c
Yom Kippur, 104
Yom Kippur, war of, 50, 51c

Z

Zebulun, tribe of, 25
Zacharia, 97
Zin, desert of, 84c
Zion, 42
Zionism, 11c, 125, 128
Ziun, 42
Zoan, 22
Zorobabel, 28c

ILLUSTRATION CREDITS

Antonio Attini/Archivio White Star: pages 1, 10 bottom, 11 top right, 57 top left, 58 top right, 59 center, 60 center right, 64 left, 67 top, 68 top, 72 center and bottom left, 74 bottom left, 78 top right, 96 top, 97 top and center, 98 top left, 100 left, 102 top right, 103 top, 104 bottom left, 107 bottom right, 108 top right, 119, 128 top.
Marcello Bertinetti/Archivio White Star: pages 8 top right, 56 top left, 57 center, 60 center left, 69 top, 70-71, 71 top, 80 top left, 99, 103 bottom, 104 top right, 104 center bottom left, 106 top, 106 bottom, 107 top right, 115-118, 120 bottom left, 122 top left, 124-125, 126 bottom, 128 bottom, 129 top, 131 bottom.
AKG Photo: pages 21, 22, 22-23, 24-25, 25 top, 26 left, 27 top, 28 bottom left, 29, 30-31, 31 bottom, 34 left, 36 top, 36 left, 40-41, 41 top, 42, 42-43, 43 center and bottom, 44, 45, 46 bottom, 46-47, 47 center, 47 bottom, 48 center and bottom, 48-49, 50 left, 52 center.
Felipe Alcoceba: pages 102 top right, 104 bottom right, 114, 120 bottom right.
The Ancient Art Architecture Collection: pages 28 top left, 31 top.
Archivio Publiphoto Olympia: pages 49 top, 51 top, 51 center bottom, 51 bottom right, 52 bottom, 53 top and center.
UPI/Corbis/Bettmann: pages 47 top, 48 top, 52 top.
Biblioteque National de France: page 34 right (Ms. 9087 Fol. 85).
Bodleian Library: pages 38-39 (Ms. Pococke 375 Fol. 123V-124R).
Leu Borodulin/Asap: page 122 center left.
The Bridgeman Art Library: page 41 bottom.
Library of Congress: pages 2-7.
E. T. Archive: pages 20, 24 left, 28 top right, 30 bottom.
Mary Evans Picture Library: pages 25 bottom, 26-27, 27 bottom, 28 bottom left, 33 right, 36-37, 38 bottom, 40 bottom, 43 top.
Gigliola Foschi/Focus Team: page 109.
Dino Fracchia/Realy Easy Star: pages 126-127.
G. P. O./Asap: pages 50-51, 51 center top, 51 bottom left.
Cesare Gerolimetto: pages 62 center, 66 bottom, 66-67, 68 bottom, 74-75, 76-77, 77 center, 82, 84 top, 92 top, 97 bottom, 98 bottom left, 104 center top right, 104 top right, 106 center, 113, 120 top and center right, 122 right, 128 center, 131 top.
Yaniv Golan/Alamy: page 121.
Itamar Grinberg: pages 8 top left, 8-9, 9, 10 top and center, 10-11, 11 top left, 12, 13, 14-15, 16-17, 54-55, 55 top left, 56 top right, 56-57, 57 bottom, 58 top left, 58-59, 59 top and bottom, 60 top, 60 bottom left, 61, 62 top, 62-63, 63 top, 64 top right, 66 top, 68 center, 68-69, 70 top and center, 72 top left, 72 right, 73, 74 top and center right, 75, 76 top, 77 top and bottom, 78 left, 78 center and bottom right, 79, 80, 80-81, 81 top right, 82-83, 83 top, 84 bottom, 84-85, 85 top, 86-87, 88, 89, 90, 91, 92 center and bottom, 92-93, 93 top, 96-97, 108 top left, 110 top and bottom, 111, 112, 113 left and right, 120 top left, 121, 122 top left, 123, 130 top left.
AVI Hirschfeld/Asap: pages 108 bottom left, 110 center.
Hanan Isachar/Asap: page 131 top.
Collection of Israel Antiquites Authority/Israel Museum, Jerusalem/David Harris: pages 18 top, 19 top left, 19 bottom, 32 bottom, 54 top, 63 bottom, 70 bottom.
Chip Hires/Gamma: page 53 bottom.
Koninkligke Bibliöteek/The Hague: page 37.
Vladimir Judin/Mary Evans Picture Library: page 46 top.
Italo Monetti: page 94 top and bottom left.
Garo Nalbandian/Asap: pages 54 bottom, 100 right.
Photo Garo Nalbandian: pages 3-6, 55 top right, 100-101, 105, 107, 108 center right, 128-129, 130 top right, 136.
Vincenzo Paolillo: page 94 center left.
Sergio Quaglia: pages 94 top right, 95.
Zev Radovan: pages 18 bottom, 19 top right, 23, 32-33, 33 bottom left, 35, 39, 60 bottom right, 64 bottom right, 65.
Roberto Rinaldi: page 94 bottom right.
Nitzan Shorer/Asap: page 127 top.
Talby/Asap: page 131 center.
Ag. Visa: page 100 top left.

136 Fluttering over Jerusalem, the Israeli flag seems to declare the importance that this city has for the whole country. Jerusalem was also the city dreamed about and invoked for centuries by Jews spread around the world by the diaspora. The natural attachment of Jews to this city is shown by the desire expressed in the traditional saying repeated each year during the Easter meal: "This year here, next year in Jerusalem".

Map by Betty Vandone